SORTIES

SORTIES

JAMES DICKEY

LOUISIANA STATE UNIVERSITY PRESS
Baton Rouge

Copyright © 1971 by James Dickey

All Rights Reserved

Printed in the United States of America

Published by arrangement with Doubleday & Company, Inc.

Louisiana Paperback Edition, 1984

ISBN 0-8071-1140-6

Library of Congress Cataloging in Publication Data

Dickey, James.
  Sorties.

  I. Title.
[PS3554.I32S6   1984   818'.5403   [B]   83-24421
ISBN 0-8071-1140-6 (pbk.)

To Maxine

CONTENTS

ACKNOWLEDGMENTS

Grateful acknowledgment is made to the following for permission to reprint their material:

"Contemporary Poetry" reprinted from *The Self as Agent* edited by J. MacMurray, 1953, by permission of Humanities Press, Inc., Atlantic Highlands, N.J. 07716.

"The Son, the Cave, and the Burning Bush" reprinted from *The Young American Poets* edited by Paul Carroll Copyright © 1968 by Follett Publishing Company. Used by permission.

"Edward Arlington Robinson," Copyright © 1969 by The New York Times Company. Reprinted by permission.

"The Great American Poet" Copyright © 1968 by The Atlantic Monthly Company, Boston, Mass. Reprinted with permission.

Excerpts from *The Distinctive Voice: Twentieth Century American Poetry* edited by W. J. Martz Copyright © 1966 by Scott, Foresman and Company. Reprinted by permission of the publisher.

"Fever 103°" by Sylvia Plath, Copyright © 1963 by Ted Hughes, from *Ariel* by Sylvia Plath. Reprinted by permission of Harper & Row.

"It Was in Vegas" by James Cunningham reprinted from *The Collected Poems and Epigrams of J. V. Cunningham* © 1971, Swallow Press. Reprinted with the permission of Ohio University Press.

"Rome" by James Cunningham reprinted from *The Collected Poems and Epigrams of J. V. Cunningham* © 1971, Swallow Press. Reprinted with the permission of Ohio University Press.

"Approaching Winter" by Robert Bly reprinted from *Silence in the Snowy Fields*, Wesleyan University Press, Copyright © 1962 by Robert Bly, by permission of the author.

"Next Day" by Randall Jarrell, reprinted with permission of The Macmillan Company from *The Lost World*, Copyright © 1963, 1965 by Randall Jarrell. Originally appeared in *The New Yorker*.

SORTIES

PART I
─────────
Journals

You cannot feel your own blood run. You can feel the pulse, but not what the pulse does: not what the pulse is for.

I am a great reader and admirer of journals, and I wonder how this particular one will turn out. Surely I am not likely to say anything scandalous or private in it, except maybe my opinions of various writers and personalities. I remember reading in one of the journals of Julien Green that he thought that his journal had turned into some kind of monster which was eating himself and his talent alive; that he devoted so much time to it and bled off so much of his energy into it that it seriously crippled him as a creative writer. I intend nothing like this in my case; the journal, if such it is, will be simply a catchall, and will contain everything from meditations on the sublime to laundry lists.

It is very odd to me that the subject of masturbation and the *fact* of masturbation are as laughed at and as reviled subjects as they are. Poor Alex Portnoy, for example, is driven not only just about crazy by it, but onto the psychiatrist's couch, which is worse. It is generally assumed that this is a shameful practice, and that we must all join together in condemning it and laughing at it whenever we find out that somebody else indulges in it. How absurd this is! It seems to me one of the most profound forms of self-communication and even self-communion. At no other time do the true and deep sensual images of the mind appear so vividly as under that kind of stimulus. It is the way the mind operates in this kind of *extremis* that tells more about what we are than anything else possibly could. Part of this is illustrated in the famous New York joke of the couple waking up in bed and one saying to the other "I'll tell you whom I was thinking about if you'll tell me whom you were thinking about." That is not so funny as we might think. The phantom women of the mind—I speak from the man's standpoint only—are a great deal more important than any real women could ever possibly be. They represent the Ideal, and as such are indestructible. It is quite arguable that poor mortal perishable women are as dust before these powerful and sensual creatures of the depths of one's being. I believe that no one can understand what it is to live a human life without understanding this, at least to some small degree.

In Stegner's book *The Sound of Mountain Water* there is the following marvelous passage: "It took some time to find a New Mexican gas station that did not advertise serpents; but when we found it and stopped to fill our tank, we asked the young man how come he felt he didn't need reptiles in his business. He told us he was just starting out, hadn't really got going yet, but did have his eye on some nice specimens. They were part of the stock of the cobra wholesaler down the road, the one whose signs had sheltered us from the wind all the way from Albuquerque. This man had, in the free spirit of trade, supplied cobras and boas, as well as lesser Ophidia, to stations as far away as Kansas. He was a real go-getter and strictly aboveboard, the boy said. If he advertised 'See the deadliest living serpent. Alive! Alive! Alive!' and his cobra died that night, he'd be right out there taking his sign down."

The body is the one thing you cannot fake. It is what it is, and it does what it does. It also fails to do what it cannot do. It would seem to me that people would realize this, especially men.

Why is the gouge-wound more terrifying to everyone than any other? Why is a wound with an ice pick, so small and so deep, so much more terrifying than a slash, in which much blood flows? Why is an ice pick so much more horrifying to anyone than a straight razor? I think it is because one realizes how fatally easy it is to enter the human body deeply and fatally with a relatively simple, edgeless implement than with something more elaborate.

What I want to do most as a poet is to charge the world with vitality: with the vitality that it already has, if we could rise to it. This vitality can be expressed in the smallest thing and in the largest; from the ant heaving at a grain of sand to the stars straining not to be extinguished.

Read the several pages of Oscar Wilde on the grave of John Keats in Rome. Very touching. If I were to go again to Rome and seek to find the grave of Keats, I would follow Oscar Wilde's instructions rather than engage the services of a guide. Strange pilgrimage, this. Indeed.

As one ages: it is thought that the worst enemy of the aging process is the mirror. This is not true at all. After all, when one looks in the mirror, one is not really so much different from the same self in the same mirror yesterday. No; the real striker of terror to the heart of the individual human being is not the mirror at all, as devastating as its revelations may be. The death-dealing agent in human life is the photograph of oneself from years back; many years, or a few years. You look at it, and you know you are going to die.

It is a marvelous thing, this having a house full of books. Something crosses the mind—a flash of light, some connection, some recognition—and one simply rises from one's chair and goes, as though by predestination, to that book, to that poem.

The symbolism in advertising. For example the various advertisements for automobiles attempting, in the most completely unconvincing way, to compare their particular model of automobile to an animal, usually a predatory animal. This is thought to suggest speed, beauty, and even a kind of *savagery* on the road, all of which qualities are supposed to be desirable, either in the consciousness or the unconsciousness of the people who might be expected to buy the automobile. In fact, these associations do nothing of the kind. I doubt if it can be *shown* that anyone ever bought one of these cars because the association had made any impression at all on them. If there has been any impression, it is only a kind of a guilty feeling on the part of the prospective consumer, in the degradation of the animal.

Why is the sense of starting over so important to me? But whenever I catch myself thinking in an uncensored way, I am always in a room in Barcelona, or Florence, or in the lower quarter of Paris, and there I see myself, no matter what my age, no matter even if it is my current forty-six, as a rugged, healthy young fellow just starting out, just having come to this city, just having come to this room, expecting something fabulous to happen as soon as I step out, or someone wonderful to knock on the door, and speak to me in a language I cannot understand.

Contemporary criticism of poetry: far too much is made of far too little. The critic is attempting to be more ingenious and talented than the poem, and stands on his head to be original: that is, to *invent* an originality for the poems that can come to them only through him.

Single comment on the readings and public styles of people like Allen Ginsberg, Robert Bly with his serape, and other curiosities: if you can really write, you don't need to dress up funny.

I enjoy the sense of being purified, cleansed. And I feel this even in a very simple personal operation like shaving. Robert Lowell says that he likes the "sheer of shaving." But that is not what I like. I like the fact that in this operation my face becomes, if only for a very short time, my own.

The reasons for suicide are usually thought to be many, most of them having to do with failed relationship to experience, to the world. Sometimes this is the case, of course, but there is another factor which is much more important than this one. One desires to get away from one's own mind; to be relieved, in some kind of permanent way, of *that*. This is the reason for the suicide of so many writers and intellectuals and artists. They have thought, when younger, that the excited, deep, associational kind of mind would bring them to the earthly paradise. But it is not so: the place is a hell. Believe me, it is better to be stupid and ordinary.

In the one love scene in *Death's Baby Machine*, which should be sensitive and imaginative and deeply sensual, Cahill asks Ellen where she learned all these things, and she tells him, quite simply, that Joel taught her. Cahill then says, "I wonder where *he* learned them?" And she says, "I asked him the same thing, and he said he just imagined them all."

Instead of Cahill, consider the possibility of calling the protagonist Vine: Frank Vine; Joel Vine.

The difference between Joel and the student revolutionaries of today is that he has a positive *goal*—or he thinks he does—that the revolt will lead to. This is the thing that I am going to have to figure out. It is the most fascinating part of the book, and I have only an inkling of what it is to be. But it will be completely different from the way men have ever lived on the earth before. I must give hints about this utopian concept of Joel's; enough to make the reader think that such a system might be better than anything any of us have ever had. Concentrate on this more than on the revolt.

Thomas Wolfe cannot *fix* it. He can talk about it, around it, above it, below it, to the side of it, but he cannot *fix* it: he cannot phrase it.

Something I got from Mark Twain: the prose of writers like John Updike might be called cakewalking prose.

Marilyn Monroe was a masturbation-fantasy of bellboys; Grace Kelly of bank executives.

The thing that I utterly detest: the writing and talking of literary razzmatazz. A great deal of poetry is written in this idiom today; this is not the real, deep thing that we all should be trying for.

One must be able to distinguish between real perception and literary sophistry. I read in Conrad Aiken's *Ushant* that everyone is floating upward "towards that vast, that outspread sheet of illuminated music, which is the world." Now who on God's earth has ever experienced the world —that is, the *world*—as a "sheet of illuminated music"? That is what I refer to as the literary syndrome: saying something fine, but very untrue to experience. It is, in a word, literary sophistry, and I am sure sick to death of that, as we all should be.

I don't like the locked-in quality of formalist verse. The only reason for writing verse of this sort is to attempt to come at an effect of inevitability. There are lots of

other kinds of inevitability than this, and the best of
these do not have the sense of claustrophobia that
formalistic verse has. Writers like Yvor Winters insist
that there is a *compression* in formalist verse that any
other kind of verse—say, open-form verse—cannot
possibly have. This is true, if you look at poetry from
Winters' point of view. But there are plenty of other
points; the human imagination is wide—very wide indeed.

I want, mainly, the kind of poetry that opens out, instead
of closes down.

An extremely new and productive concept of playing the
guitar, one which is possible to me now after about ten
years of playing. This is the concept of phrasing. That is,
to make the song, and the moments of the song, the chord
changes, the other technical aspects, and so on, your *own*.
Nothing could be more important than this, and nothing
is. The main thing is to experiment, not to be caught in a
routine, mechanical interpretation of any guitar method, or
anything you have learned from someone else, but to take
the whole business over. It is fine to learn, but the main
thing is to *move* on the song, to create your own rhythm,
your own urgencies, and, above all, your own phrasing.
Americans are kind of embarrassed to be "theatrical," and
to put too much emphasis on this, that, or the other thing,
being in love with a mechanical perfection. But folk
music—any music—provides an outlet where the individual
rendition is still important. This is something that must
and should be utilized.

Play with confidence, power, and relaxation. If one can
add abandon to that, one has the thing as it should be
had.

To that, add precision.

Phrase it, *phrase* it. One cannot work too much on such a thing.

In the new novel that I am now projecting the main technical difficulty is going to be the one of making the personality of the dead son both enigmatic and interesting. There have been some novels—including popular novels like *Rebecca*—that have used devices similar to this, but whether in a popular novel or a so-called "literary" work such as this one the rule would seem to be this: that the personality of the dead person around which the action of the other people in the book rotates has got to be in some way deserving of interest even if the person is dull. His very dullness must be interesting and revelatory. This factor poses the main technical difficulty of the book. Of course what really matters in the end is not so much the personality of the dead son as the change and revelation and in a sense the rebirth of the father, as he discovers himself in his forever unmeetable son. The indications of his own character in the character of his son must be done with extreme delicacy, and not done with the kind of obviousness that such a treatment would probably invite. I don't mean here to be talking about "inherited" traits in the son, but will try to work with the situation that the son has lived with the father and the boy's mother up until the age of about five or six, and that during these formative years the father has planted the seeds of behavior and attitude in the boy which flower monstrously and marvelously later on, years after the father has last laid eyes on this son. So what the father encounters, then, in these reminiscences of his boy, are enormously exaggerated characteristics which are present in himself in other forms. The upshot of this, in the end, is that, though not an unusually intelligent man, he understands himself, in middle age, a great deal better than he ever has done before. His conduct does not change a great deal—though it does change some—but he understands the actions that he perpetrates, and the way he treats others and the way he treats himself. It is as though by the events of this week or so at the primary air training base, he has undergone a kind of painful and practical and chance psychoanalysis of himself by means of information that other people have given him about his son. It is as though he were a researcher gathering material for a biography never to be written, but whose ultimate result is his own cleansing, and to some extent his rejuvenation. In addition to this I would like to have the sense of flying restored, in this period of high-speed jet travel. This is a very important part of the book's intention: of its *physical* intention. These are primary trainers—that is, they are very low-speed and tremulous aircraft, and, except for the instructors, are flown by people who have flown little or none before. The father, for example, has never been off the ground, and when he gets into the aircraft with the boy's rebellious-minded country instructor, it is as though he were taking off in one of the old aircraft of the Wright brothers. I want this *precariousness* of flight restored. It is going to be awfully difficult to do this, I know, but I believe it can be done. In other words, I would like to convey the sense of flight as it was almost at the very beginning of itself, when everything about it was miraculous and dangerous and exhilarating. There might be a point in the novel, for example, when one of the boys who has just soloed describes what it felt like to him. I should somewhere or other come by an old Stearman PT tech manual, so that I can get straight on a number of the operational procedures that I have forgotten about. I could write the novel without this, by concentrating on the father's ignorance of air technology, much as I got around the intricacies of white water canoeing in *Deliverance* and my unfamiliarity with the technical, botanical, naturalistic aspects of trees and rocks by making such unfamiliarity part of the effectiveness of the presentation of the central character.

But if I do use a cadet, he would most pridefully talk
about flying from the technical part of it, and if I do
that section of the novel in that manner, I will need to
know more about flying a Stearman than I recall. But the
main thing here is to restore this sense of the
precariousness and the miraculousness of flight. The whole
book should be close to aircraft; should be surrounded by
the sounds and the feel and the presence of these very
low-speed World War I-type aircraft that boys are
learning to fly so that they may later fly other more
deadly and efficient machines in the war. But this sense of
flight, in which every automobile on the road, every road
itself, every lake and cornfield and house and forest and
fence and individual tree become transfigured by distance,
is the most important of the psychological states of being
which I wish to produce—or reproduce—in the book.
Very few people have ever written well about flying,
although there is hardly a more written-about subject in
modern literature. But there is this *physical* sense of
flying, this angelic view, this bird-like and yet very
man-like position in the sky where things on the ground
shrink up and are transfigured and reduced to some kind
of curious heavenly and earthly scale that men before 1900
never saw, that is important. It has been missed by most
writers about flying. Saint-Exupéry has written pretty
well of some of the aspects of flying, but one feels that
he is too obviously rapturous—and in a rather ordinary
way—about the pilot's position. I don't want my book to
do or be anything like that: obviously "poetic." What I *do*
want is the sense of transfiguration and danger and
precariousness and a certain kind of timorous and
unlooked-for glory. This is a new attitude for the body,
one men have had only a few years: to be positioned,
moving, in space, and to have the view either from a
Stearman PT-17 or from a rocket ship: these are new
attitudes and conditions for the body, new dangers and
new ecstasies. I will contrive to say something about this

not from the standpoint of the space pilot at all—but
something of the same feeling will be implied as part of
any new effort of men to hurl their bodies into the air,
or into space—but from the standpoint of very primitive
aircraft. Every one of these boys at the primary training
base feels as though he himself has discovered air, and is
the first to live in it. The son, of course, has died in it:
in very peculiar circumstances; that is, flying over a forest
fire.

I must get from Longmans a list of the titles of books by
Richard Jefferies. *The Story of My Heart* is one of the
really good books, and is very close to what I feel about
existence. It is simply a book of meditations on nature
and on one's relationship to it. Jefferies earned most of his
living during his short life by writing explicitly on nature,
and not meditating upon it at all. I would like to have
more of an idea of how he wrote about the English
landscape, the flowers, and the animals, for *The Story of
My Heart* gives very little notion of this at all. It is just
mostly about Jefferies lying out in the sun on an English
hillside and feeling himself taken up into the cosmos. In a
way, this is kind of laughable, and someone like Auden
would think it intolerably egotistical and romantic. But I
am not built that way. The book has a very powerful
effect upon me, because I am an essentially emotional
writer, just as I am a very emotional person. That is
just the way it is with me, and it is a situation not to be
apologized for, but to be used.

Bo Bexley has written to ask if I would be willing to take
on his four children in case he and his wife are killed. I
am answering that I will do this. I would not mind in
the slightest, though I realize how much difficulty and how
much trouble it would be to raise that many children.
Since Bo is rich, and since he is setting up all kinds of
trust funds and things to take care of the financing of

such a situation, the money problem shouldn't be
difficult. But I would do it anyway. First of all I like
Bo's children very much, and secondly Bo would do the
same thing for me, I know. He is that way.

Possibility of three months in Europe next summer with
Tom and Patsy. This is important: It could be the
regeneration of your brother's wife.

Get back to linguistic studies. Translate all of Lucien
Becker, beginning with the very first poems. Let me try
to sight-read one of these now, and see how it sounds in
a very rough draft. I'll just do this very literally and
then refer to it a little later on when I want to change
things around and make the English a little better. This is
the first poem from Becker's first book *Le Monde sans
Joie.*

The wind rises suddenly from a pond
Where in places smash and are confused
The murderesses of the night
And those more profound of the sun.

The Earth is cold and enormous at its waking
Like a room without a fire
I am alone at the edge of my weary mouth;
A cigarette is breathing in place of me.

I hasten toward a corridor that has no end
Where the doors make tunnel-like stains,
Where the shadows brush against each other without suffering
And where the walls are dirty and eternal.

The light seems heavy and vaulted
Under a world without miracle, nor gaiety.
In the nudity of the blood which turns in me,
I breathe the same cold pebble.

Others will live my life in their turn,
Solitary between the high walls of the heart.

Only the head changes its look;
From the heart leaves the same plant of despair.

Though it is not an outstanding poem of Becker's, it is
typical of him: the quatrain form, the unemphasized,
poignant, simple diction, and the continued emphasis on
futility. Though many poets have written about futility,
despair, and the occasional ecstasies of love and
love-making, I know of no poet anywhere who does this
with such divine simplicity and naturalness as he does.
People should know about this, and I will try to get
some of Becker into English, so that they will.

Yesterday went out with Cal Winton and shot both sides
of the archery range. I shot the Hoyt Pro-Medalist, and
recalibrated what I use for a sight. The Hoyt bow is the
best bow I have ever owned or ever shot. I am not sure
it is as fast as I previously believed, but it is mighty fast.
I had to come up about five yards or between five and
ten yards on the eighty-yard shot, but that really is not
so much at that distance. The Howatt bow is also very
good, and I must get the sight zeroed in on it, and see
which is the faster bow. But I still believe, whether it is
faster or not, the Hoyt bow is the better one for me to
use. First of all, it draws very easily and smoothly, the
consequence being that I can get the arrow off the rest
much easier and don't have to struggle so much. This in
turn means that I can hold on a point—that is, on the
target—without working so hard to get the arrow off. I
shot 194 on the new side, where all the easy targets are
together, and 185 on the old side, which is a little bit
harder, though not much. I was very satisfied with this
performance, for it brings me back up to tournament level,
if I can maintain it, and hopefully, improve it. It also
means that my hunting capacity is much furthered, and it
is a nice feeling to know that you could take on any
big game animal and be confident that you could hit it
in a vital area.

One more note in connection with archery: I am forever done with helical-fletched arrows. I must take these four green helicals I have to Skip and have him redo them and add eight more matching arrows to them with a normal four-fletch. Since these helicals I have are 1816s, they should shoot very well out of either the Hoyt or the Howatt bow, and give me an extra set of 1816s. However, in the future, and judging from the results yesterday, I believe it would be best for me to shoot twenty-eight-inch thin-walls: that is to say, 1913s.

Do something about the German language. What little I have been able to decipher of that curious tongue is enormously exciting. Though not a born linguist, I have a good memory and can pick up a good deal of the language very quickly, though mechanically, in a short time. German is interesting to me because the manner in which words are combined, and the manner in which verb forms—that is to say, action words—are combined with other forms like adverbs and nouns, is extremely interesting and exciting. I have no doubt at all that something of this sort could be done in English, and it would have the effect of creating a very expressive new approach for poetry, or even for prose. It is important that I look into this; I have been promising myself to do it for a long time, and now I will do it.

Italian and Spanish are much easier languages to learn than German, because they are so much closer to English than German is. Anyone with a fairly large vocabulary in English, a certain amount of intelligence, and a rudimentary knowledge of word derivations can read either Spanish or Italian without ever having had, as they say, "a course in it." Of course, a good deal of the subtlety of the language would be lost, inevitably. But the *gist* of it would be more or less obvious; that is, such a person could read the newspaper and gather from it what was going on. I have done this myself, so I know it to be a fact.

Try to get out at least three or four letters a day. Or five. Five would be better. There is no telling what that extra letter might bring into being.

Get back on a day-to-day schedule and stick to it to the very letter of the law. Your mistake for so many years is to set up impossible work schedules, and if something intervenes, as it almost always does, your attitude has been that if you can't do it all, you won't do any. This is not only very childish but very destructive of your work. The point is that if you have any time at all, you should do whatever the top-priority thing to be done at that time is. There won't be many days when you can go through the whole schedule, when you can get in three hours on the guitar, and the rest. But playing the guitar for fifteen or twenty minutes a day is a lot better than not even picking it up. It is also better to get off one rather than five letters because that is one real letter, and if you depended on the five-letter schedule, and didn't write any letters if you couldn't write five, it would be, as it has been in the past, disastrous. So do *something*, even if you have to assign priorities. The whole point is to do *some* writing, some guitar playing, and something physical every day, no matter what. That is the only way to live, and to get your work done.

Biography of Hart Crane by John Unterecker. First of all, write to Unterecker and tell him how good the book is, and how thorough and invaluably detailed it is. Louis Simpson, a very mediocre poet in my opinion, has done the most inadequate job of reviewing the book that could imaginably be done. If it were not against my policy, and more or less against my personality, I would surely call his hand on this. But I think it would be better to speak

to Unterecker about it than to go into the tiresome
business of having a public row with Simpson, though
I would surely win without as much trouble as might
be gone to, were the opponent better. In reading the
biography of Crane, I am struck by the fact that Crane
was devoted to the arts in such a wholehearted way
that he seems to have had no other interests at all.
Although naturally a very responsive person, and
sometimes excited by such things as crowds in cities,
airplanes taking off, factories, and the like, it is very
obvious that he looked on these things not as entities
but as material for poetry. This attitude goes against the
grain for me, although I admire some of Crane's work
very much. But the trouble with Crane was that he was
an aesthete. Seldom have I encountered a life more
completely bound up in the arts, so that his bouts with
drinking and with sexual excess are hardly more than
adjuncts to his continued preoccupation with the aesthetic
life, and more particularly with movements, with artistic
manifestoes, with artists and their problems, with
theorizing about poetry, and so on. As he writes about
these things, he is very good indeed. I would not have
thought that such an avowed aesthete as Crane would
ever interest me very much. Yet seldom have I
encountered such a lively, vivid mind within such a
narrow framework. His theories of poetry, of art, of
photography, and of the whole world he chose to deal
with are fascinating. His judgments of other writers, such
as Sherwood Anderson, are devastatingly accurate, and
very original. It is a measure of Crane's success that his
influence could be so powerfully felt by a person like
myself, so completely different from him in temperament
except in one or two regards: mainly, a kind of induced
responsiveness.

Crane's is one of the few lives that one can get
absolutely caught up in. Elizabeth Hardwick is very

good on this, in a brief piece in her book *A View of My Own*, but she is quite wrong when she says that Crane's letters are free of artiness. They *are* artiness, though much more in a good sense than the bad. As Crane's friend, Sam Loveman says, Crane was always the artist. There is something oppressive about this to me, even in a figure I like so much as I do Crane. Keats is oppressive in somewhat the same way, but in his letters he does not contrive to give the impression of being closed off in the world of Art in an absolute sense as Crane does. His responsiveness was much different from Crane's, and included a very great deal more.

Play around with the idea of getting an electric typewriter. Would this help things, *really?*

Get in some kind of touch with Roy Noble in California. He is into me for $150 and owes me a guitar. Guitar players will mortgage their souls for instruments that they can play well. Also, I would like to do whatever I can for Roy, because I very much believe in the handcraft tradition and would like to do something about preserving it and encouraging it in this country.

It is time for me to pay a kind of debt to the advertising industry, even if only in my mind. It is important that I was in advertising, and it is also important that I was in it for as long as I was. I can now go up to a book designer, for example, and argue from a commercial standpoint, or from a design standpoint, as to what would be effective in the design. I can see this operating in the jacket design for the new book of poems, and for the proposed design for the novel. It is foolish to say that these things are not important; they are *very* important. I remember when I was first working in advertising, or rather when I was in the middle of my time in advertising, I suggested to Wesleyan that they do something with one of Matisse's cut-out angel-forms for the cover of *Drowning with Others*. The art director, Harry Rich, took up the idea immediately and produced an outstandingly beautiful cover. This would not have been the cover if I had not been conversant with Matisse's work in this genre, and if I had not been thinking a good deal about design elements in connection with some advertising that I was at that time producing.

I tried hard, some of the time, to learn what advertising had to teach me. I make no bones of the fact that at one time I hoped to make a great deal of money from it, which Hart Crane, another ad man, was congenitally unable to do. But the main thing was to open up, emotionally, to American business, and to let that develop whatever there was in me to be developed by it. If one cannot assess the value of certain actions and certain conditions to one's developing personality, one is in a state of stasis or retardation. It is absolutely necessary to be honest with one's self about these things. My feeling is this: that whatever adds a cubit to one's stature, either psychologically or physically, is worth it. There is a kind of personality that nothing at all can change; that cannot grow, cannot alter, and can never be anything but the limited being that it is. There is another kind of personality, such as Keats, or to some extent Hart Crane, that can learn, literally, from anything. This kind of personality welcomes change, because it seems to lead somewhere. It is a matter of what Henry James called "accessibility to experience"; the quality is to some extent natural to the person, and to some extent encouraged, and sometimes he sets out to find ways to encourage it. I do this, though I imagine I was born with some kind of extra sensitivity to things. But that is hard to determine. I sometimes think that sensitivity, so called, is partly a capacity to be hurt by things, and partly intelligence both natural and cultivated. I also think that memory is to a very large degree connected with the capacity of the person to receive impressions, and the more mysterious capacity he has to retain these, simply because, for some reason or other, they *mean* something to him. *That* quality I do have, and to a very marked degree indeed. Things matter to me; big things and little things. I feel for them in some manner, and so I remember them. My whole poetic work, pretty much, has been made of such memories.

On the guitar, I would like very much to do something to implement my knowledge of musical structure. It is amazing how one thing can lead to another; how an interest in one aspect of music—say, simply the mechanical aspects of playing an instrument—can lead to others. Once one has a repertoire of a few chords and a few songs, it is almost inevitable that in some way one begins to explore the *structure* of music. A simple incident, like walking into a music store, looking at the music books offered, and buying one that has to do with harmony, can lead to a lifelong fascination with the permutations and combinations of musical tones. I welcome this kind of thing, myself. If I had nine or ten lives, I would like nothing better than to spend one of them exploring musical possibilities, particularly in the idioms of folk music and jazz, but perhaps moving out from these into more "serious" music as well.

The compartments of the day and the night are things which I must understand better than I have done up to the present time. It is obvious that one does things better at some times in the day—or night—than others, but for any given day this may not be true. There is only a limited degree to which one can systematize, here. But I had a lot rather write poetry early, when I am enthusiastic about doing it, than when I come to it after having done other things which have tired me out during the day. On the other hand, I had rather write letters at night, because I know I don't have to be thinking at the intensity and at the level that poetry demands, that I can make some mistakes, and that the main thing is the physical effort of communication, rather than any attempt to be "literary." I hope no one ever collects my letters; they are not very good. I want my energy, insofar as writing is concerned, to go into things I set more store by. It might be argued that the letters of almost any writer are worth preserving, but if I tried to write letters like Hart Crane or like Keats or like Thomas Gray or like any of the writers of "Great Letters," I sincerely believe that this would bleed off the verbal and nervous energy that I need for poetry and for novels.

Why is World War I so fascinating to people these days? There are various possibilities, but I am not sure any of them is satisfactory. I personally believe that it is because, in a world continually at war, *that* war is the worst war, as far as the individual soldier was concerned, that has ever been fought. There is never likely to be a war that is so degrading, so dirty, so heartlessly tiresome and confusing and confined than that one. You read these memoirs of trench warfare like Robert Graves's *Goodbye to All That*, or David Jones's *In Parenthesis*, or that much neglected masterpiece of a little book of Thomas Boyd's, *Through the Wheat*, and you realize just how horrible war can be. I saw some of this in the Pacific, but in comparison to the trench warfare of World War I, even the jungle war of New Guinea and the Philippines—or, for that matter, Vietnam—is comparatively easy. Most of the soldiers now are much better supplied, much better cared for, and much better fed than those poor people floundering around in the slime and the shit and the corpses and rats under the flare lights and enfilades of No Man's Land and of the trenches.

Edmund Blunden's *Undertones of War* is a very good
record of this, as is *All Quiet on the Western Front,*
book which I believe, as Harvey Swados does, is a
masterpiece of some sort. Surely it is very fortunate in its
English rendering; though I don't know German very well,
I'd be willing to bet that the book is better in English
than it is in the original. Anyway, it surely ought to be
read. Some people have talked about *All Quiet on the
Western Front* as they would talk about, say, a novel by
Henry James. They fault it for its lack of characterization.
But what seems to me to be good about the book, as an
account of warfare, is this very simplicity, and the fact
that the author is not forever analyzing the characters and
the inner relationships of the people in the story. We
know enough about Himmelstoss, about Tjaden, about
Westhus, to make them vivid for us without further
commentary. I, for example, would not like to have a
long, and perhaps long-winded, analysis of Westhus'
upbringing and so on: that is, I would be very much
opposed to having had the author do with his characters
what Norman Mailer attempted to do in *The Naked and
the Dead,* a vastly inferior book.

Remember to take with you to New York the poems
of Yevtushenko that Doubleday wants you to translate.
I don't have a great deal of enthusiasm for this project,
to tell you the truth, but I believe I will be able to do a
little more with it, even though I don't know Russian,
than has been done up to this point. I am interested to
find out how this will turn out as an experiment, for this
kind of "translating" is very prevalent now, and I might
as well be doing it as some of the other people who are
doing it.

I am pondering writing an introduction to Allan Seager's
Collected Stories, but this means that I must read them
all. I don't mind that, and I have read most of them

anyway, but I *do* resent the loss of time that this would entail. I think I probably will do it, though, because I loved the man so much, and because he is a writer who ought to be read. He is very fortunate in having as his editor William Goyen, who likes the work as much as I do, and who is battling very hard to have it published. I will do what I can.

I wonder if it would be possible to issue a kind of one-volume collected works of Alun Lewis? Surely there is not so much work that it could not appear in one book? Question is, would people be interested enough in it to buy it and read it? I think so; I know *I* would. I wonder if one could get in touch with Gweno Lewis?

Keep writing to Tony Rossiter. He is not only a lovely human being, but a fine artist. All he lacks is a true vision. But he is in touch with nature, and in an uncommonly intimate way. The trouble with Tony as an artist is that he is somewhat derivative. He has these ecstasies over *feeling* the subject of the picture, and to hear him *write* about it you'd think that some marvelous original inscape was going to come forth. Instead, when it comes, it comes out looking like Graham Sutherland or Van Gogh. This is too bad, but it may be that Tony will work out of this derivative mode, and get into the originality that he so much deserves to have, for there can have been few painters in the whole history of art so devoted to the *act* of painting as he is. Anyway, I've commissioned a seascape from him, and will hang it no matter what it looks like. I genuinely like the small picture of his I have bought, *Storm-struck Corn*, and I believe that if Tony were to go more for the shaggy, convulsed aspect of things, he would do better than he is doing on still lifes and other subjects of that genre. But keep in touch with him I must and should do; seldom have I encountered another person that I would be so unwilling to lose.

Get some cheap water colors and play around with painting and making some sketches. It will be discouraging, surely, for you have no artistic talent at all. But one should work at least *some* in a medium which one so much admires as I do painting. I might do all right with color; it is *line* that would throw me, I'm quite sure. The only chance I might ever have to do any interesting work would be if my elbow slipped, or something, and produced a line that had a kind of chance effectiveness. But there is nothing to systematize, nothing at all to build on. Do it anyway.

What is this fascination in me for attempting and spending a great deal of time on activities for which I have no natural ability? I wanted to be a sprinter when I was a track man, when in point of fact I was quite a good hurdler. I wanted to play guitar music when in fact I have no ear for music, nor any talent for it. I would like to paint, when I cannot even sign my name twice the same way. I have always been aware of this, and in some ways it is quite unfortunate. I thought for a long time that poetry would be one of these same vain endeavors, but it was not. Poetry is very easy for me, though I work at it more than most *generations* of poets work on poems. But I know, when I begin something, that it will be at least reasonably good; I have never been wrong about this, and when I transcend these limits, the really good things are born.

Read through the last book of Galway Kinnell's, and was rather disappointed. I had never read very much of his work before, although people come up to me all the time and tell me that we are similar, and Nemerov, I remember, said that his book, then up for the Pulitzer Prize, was just "a spin-off of yours." Kinnell has something of the same general orientation to nature, and so on, that I have, but his diction and his approach

are quite different from mine. For one thing, the
rhythmical structure of his poems is almost non-existent.
In a way he is a very boring writer; very limited.
But he is a sincere man; anyone can see that, and this
may be enough to interest some people in the poems
he writes. But his subject matter is very limited, and
very monotonous in the end. He is not going to be an
important figure, I am quite sure.

One of the troubles of most of the poets of my
generation, one of the reasons they seem unable to
develop beyond a certain point, is that they don't *think*
enough about what they are doing and about what they
are trying to do, and about what they hope to do in the
future. One can learn a lesson from Hart Crane in this
regard. He theorizes endlessly, and, though a good many
of the theories are rather silly ones, the great poems
could not have been written without them. I have to
spend a certain portion of every day thinking through a
number of new avenues to explore, and a certain amount
of every day exploring these. I am full of ideas about
what might be done, and I ought to be pushing out the
limits of what I have already done. I sat down the other
day to write a couple of new poems, but like most of my
things, they are *anecdote* poems; that is, they tell a
story or recount an incident. I like this approach,
obviously, but I don't think I ought to be limited to it.

I am supposed to be a kind of spokesman for spontaneity
and for the primitive quality of the human personality.
I wonder how true that is? Not how true the possibility
that I may be the—or a—spokesman for this part of the
personality, but how true spontaneity itself is? At least,
how true it is in poetry? I sometimes think that the best
definition of poetical creativity that I know is the title of
the book by the French writer who calls himself Pierre
Emmanuel, which means in English, *Poetry, Reason on*

Fire. And if that's not what his title means exactly, it's what it *ought* to mean. It seems to me that a kind of heightening of the reasoning faculty, the inducement or occurrence of a state in which the *reason* jumps back and forth making fortuitous and perhaps, under those conditions, inevitable connections, is what really happens when one is on one of those higher wave lengths of the imagination that produces genuinely new metaphors. Perhaps it is best not to speculate too much, but just let it happen. Surely, when it's happening, one can think of nothing more exciting; there is no place on Earth that one would rather be.

The poetic line is one of the enigmas of the generations and of the ages. I think one must decide what kind of line one wants, and what one wishes it to do. The decision cannot possibly be a panacea, but must function only as kind of a normative—or even illusory—principle. What I have tried to get so far is a kind of plain-speaking line in which astonishing things could be said without rhetorical emphasis. So far, that has been the best way with me. I had far rather written some of my poems than any of Hart Crane's. Necessary vanity, perhaps. And yet, Crane does things with language that never would have occurred to me to do, and they are beautiful. Where does this leave us? Only with the idea that what I have done can be and has been done, but also with the idea that I should do this and other things too. *What* other things? That will remain to be seen, but it is possible that a highly wrought and figurative language is not entirely beyond me, and might be interesting to mess around with. The "Pine" poem is very artificial, but very interesting. I could do more of this, deliberately keeping the narrative element out, or at least down, and we could then see what might be the issue of it. But the most important thing is to keep the mind open, receptive, and alert to possibilities, no matter *where* they come from.

People are very rigid about categorizing things. Someone like Robert Bly will have a slot in his mind where he will put, say, a poet like A. D. Hope. He will then proceed to drop the name of A. D. Hope in a derogatory sense, wherever he happens to be able to drop it; at cocktail parties, in print whenever he can manage it, and anywhere else possible to him. This is a very uncreative attitude, it seems to me. I have been guilty of it myself, and doubtless will be again. But that does not keep it from being uncreative. The truly creative person will look at a soap opera—universally condemned by intellectuals—and get a good deal from it. For example, he can look at the furniture in the set of the soap opera, and he will have a pretty good idea as to what is *considered* average, lower, or upper middle class, or whatever the people being characterized are supposed to be, life at a certain time and a certain place. No one can tell me that this is not a valuable attitude. It is only the imperceptive person, like Bly, who will condemn soap operas out of hand. One of the valuable insights of McLuhan is that he sees the particular virtues of things that other people condemn because of the opportunity to condemn them, and because they are imminently, on certain grounds, condemnable. One must go back to Matthew Arnold, and other Guardians of Taste, to realize how much of the human sensibility has been cut off by insistence on Standards. One is squarely between the horns of a dilemma, here. In a recent essay of George P. Elliott, for example, he says that the religion of California is cars. Elliott goes to stockcar races at Riverside, California, and one of the new model sports cars is driven out onto the track, and he notes a sigh of desire and excitement run through the crowd when the new model is driven around the track. To him, this is indicative of something detestable in the

American character. Why must it be detestable? In our technologically orientated society, why could this not be something like a religious experience? The trouble with intellectuals like Elliott, and like Randall Jarrell, and like many another, is that they are unreceptive to what time gives them. Their standards are essentially aesthetic standards. My own feeling is this: there should be the capacity and the elasticity in the mind of man to sit out on the side of a hill like a cave man, noting it all, being amazed by it all, and still be able to enter, perhaps with only a few scars, a technological environment, and see the possibilities—moral, aesthetic, and physical—of *that*. Why cannot this be the case? What I wish for man is a much greater elasticity, a much greater accessibility to experience, and fewer preconceptions.

I have lately been reading the posthumous notebooks of Winfield Townley Scott, and seldom have I enjoyed anything so much. Scott was a very dedicated man, and in the cause of poetry and the writing of poetry can have but few peers. On almost every page I was delighted by his good sense, his refusal to be taken in by reputation, and the general *usefulness* of what he has to say about poetry and about the business of living. I wished, time and again, that the notebooks were three or four times as long. There is almost no pretentiousness here, and every entry, just about, has *something* in it which one would wish to applaud. And yet, when one turns to Scott's poetry, the thing he mulled over and worried about and endlessly worked with, one is very much disappointed. The trouble with Scott's work, despite his lifelong preoccupation with the craft of poetry, with the small and the large details, with his attitude toward it and his method of working in it, is that there is almost nothing good to be found. One concludes from this that it is the essential commonplaceness of

Scott's mind and his general human makeup that is at
fault. No amount of work, no amount of good will,
no amount of application can compensate for the fact
that Scott has a very ordinary kind of dime-a-dozen
sensibility. If there were any justice in Heaven or on
Earth, this would not be so. But it *is* so.

On the other hand, I have just been sent for approval
or disapproval the new book of Brewster Ghiselin.
Ghiselin has been sort of in and out of poetry all his
life. This new book, *The Country of the Minotaur*,
is much like the others. Ghiselin cannot keep himself
away from philosophical and mythological themes, and
most of the poems written around these themes are
very dull and very predictable. Nevertheless, he has
a true personal relationship to a couple of kinds of
experiences. These are the sea and the desert, and when
he engages these themes in what one cannot help
thinking of as a *bodily* way, his poetry rises to rather
astonishing heights. He is one of the few poets who
understand how to use *color* in poetry, for example.
He is not a great poet, but he is a real poet, and the
best of his work will be around for a long time,
probably nurtured and prolonged in the hands of a
very few people.
    I can't think of anything of Scott's that will last. And
yet he was a very good man, and worked in a good
cause. I looked up the one review I did of him, a
longish piece on a very long poem of his called
"The Dark Sister," and discovered that I gave him a
very good report. I reread this poem, and my opinion
was very much mistaken. Yet it pleases me that Scott
died thinking that *I* thought he was a good poet, for
hadn't I said so? Maybe it is better this way than to be
Diogenes or Hegel, who, when questioned as to whether
he would save the life of his wife if he could do so by
telling a lie, thundered, "No! If my wife must die by

the truth, then let her die." I am not made of such stern stuff myself. And, by the way, what is "truth" anyway? Do I have it? Not at all. My opinion is only opinion, like everybody else's.

There is a very great deal of difference between originality and novelty.

How amazingly easy it is to defend *anything* intellectually!

I have seldom spent such a good afternoon of human time as I did a few years ago with John Simon in New York. I just happened to have a free afternoon there, and went up to John's apartment. All his electricity had been turned off for some reason, and he didn't have any ice, but that was all right, since he didn't have any liquor either. We sat around and talked about writing, and about poets. He said, "Do you know who I *really* like?" I said I hadn't any idea, thinking it would be some new French poet I hadn't heard of. Not at all. He pulled out an old book of *The Collected Poems of Andrew Young,* a rather mild English ecclesiastical poet, and read to me for two or three hours. I sat there with my mouth open. Here was the great avant-garde film critic, art critic, and literary critic reading to me from these mild good poems I hadn't known. Do you think he would have mentioned this predilection in *The New Leader* or *The Hudson Review?* Maybe not. But these things will out. I noticed that in a movie review John used a quotation from Young having to do with the poet's "racing" with the river Stour, saying that
> ". . . I lost the race;
> I could not keep so slow a pace."

This had a wonderful effect on me when I saw it. It seemed such good time spent with John, such a revelation.

I have just watched the Miss America pageant on TV, and I must say that I have seldom encountered anything so thoroughly depressing. It is all so suffocatingly bourgeois. The poor girls act like a sixty- or seventy-year-old woman's idea of how young women ought to act. What kind of briefing do these girls have to go through before the final judging? It would be very interesting to know. Who sets the standards, and thinks that such standards ought to be the ones set? Why not bikinis? Is the navel un-American?

The pre-Socratic philosophers have always fascinated me enormously. What must it have been like to be a thinker in those days, when men really *did* have the illusion that the whole composition of the universe could be reduced to one or two elements: when men really did think that they could find the answer: *the* answer, the only one? When there was no knowledge of the complicated combinations and recombinations of chemicals and atoms, and there were only a few basic laws of physics, which, as these men believed, applied to everything including the planets and the celestial bodies farther away? Human thought was reduced to a few essential laws, and the rest was brilliant speculation. But *what* speculation! It was a time when science and poetry were marvelously wedded, and we shall not see its like again.

Just by chance, in reading Mauriac's book of essays, *Second Thoughts*, I came on a quotation that might be useful in "The Indian Maiden." It is in an essay of Mauriac's on Maurice de Guérin. I don't quote it exactly as the French has it, but the gist is ". . . a woman he worshiped because in no way did he dissociate her from a universe. . . ." Whether or not I use this, it is surely the *feeling* I want for the poem.

Beginning to translate Yevtushenko. It is interesting, this: for help I have some literal translations by a Harvard

graduate student in Russian. The trouble with the
translation I am working from, however, is that there is
little of the truly startling turn of phrase that
Yevtushenko occasionally manages to come up with. From
what I am able to tell, the guts of Yevtushenko's style is
colloquialism. The best of the poems seem to be rattled
off crazily in a very engaging youthful hell-for-leather
manner. When this approach fails, the work is very
slipshod and sounds improvised in the bad sense. But the
best of Yevtushenko's work has a true *seeming*
spontaneity, and it is this quality I am trying to get, or,
if the original truly does not have this at all, to invent
for him?

I really must go ahead and push on with Spanish. In any
language that one does not know very well there are
always names which seem to hold forth a vast promise.
One almost hates to know the language better, for fear
that one will be disappointed. For example, I had an idea
that Octavio Paz is a writer I could learn a lot from, and
that I would get to like a great deal, if I could read
Spanish better. Yet I have a great fear of *getting* to know
Spanish better and discovering that Paz is nothing more
than a run-of-the-mill Mexican surrealist. But, on the other
hand, there are some names that hold forth this particular
kind of magic and are better and better the more one
knows the language in which the poems are written. Luis
Cernuda is one of these, or at least he is for me.
Vincente Aleixandre is another. These people have made of
surrealism something more than just a new literary
gimmick; they have used it to explore their own segment
of reality, and their work is very good indeed. I surely am
looking forward very much to making a deeper
acquaintance with both of them, and with whomever else
I happen to turn up in the Spanish language. This is one
of the things about the kind of literary exploration that I
like most to do: all time from the beginning of language

is available; all writers, all poems, all plays of the mind on all subjects.

Today I had a letter from Guy Coriden expressing a great deal of understanding about my inability to go to Russia this fall. However, he seems to want me to keep the project in mind, and I must talk things over with the University here to see if it would be all right for me to go next year. If the University will give me a month off, or maybe even a semester off, I will go. I would very much like to go, and I must make this clear to Coriden. I must make it clear to him also that I would want someone who speaks Russian with me at all times, even at all times of the *night*. From my experiences in traveling in Japan, it is just as well for me to admit that I am absolutely terrified of not being able to communicate with people: not being able to communicate with *anyone*. I don't want to let myself in for that again, ever.

There might be some wonderful piece of writing latent in that newspaper item I saw the other day about the Korean fellow who fell off the ship and then grabbed onto a giant sea turtle and rode him for several days before he was picked up. That is wonderful to me. What must that man have felt? What must the turtle have felt? What must they have felt together?

You could classify, I guess, in a way, the two attitudes of creative writers—or, rather, the attitudes of two kinds of creative writers—by the kinds of sports writers there are. For example, yesterday I watched Rod Laver win at Forest Hills. The next day, two kinds of journalist made their appearance. One kind talks about Laver being "bandy-legged" and refers to his left arm "like a wagon tongue." The other kind concentrates not on the rather curious physique of Laver but on his devastating ability to cover court and to hit the ball hard where he wants it to go. As far as my own position is concerned, I would be very much of the latter camp. It does not matter to me that Laver's arm which hits all those devastating shots is twice as big as the *other* arm. That is not the important thing.

The debasement of all folk styles that have ever existed in the world come to a culmination in Bobbie Gentry. What the appeal of that little rat-faced woman is I cannot imagine.

The question of vocabulary is one that has never ceased to be anything less than all-important. I don't know how many words there are that come into the language every month, every week, every day, but they probably could be counted by the dozens per day. Many of these have to do with technology. But oddly enough, all of them don't. Technological words are very interesting ones, and, except for those which deal with the most specialized technical kinds of application of human knowledge, are quite easily capable of being assimilated into poetry. In addition, a great many of these terms are wonderful: wonderfully concrete. "Setscrew," for example. We have only had the setscrew for a few dozen years. "Ecology" is a word that everyone knows now, and is interested in, and has opinions about. Whoever heard of ecology a few years back? One is constantly being bombarded by these terms, and, as a poet, one at first hasn't any real idea of how to go about acquiring them. There are two ways that they may be acquired. First is deliberately to go into the vocabularies of these special fields; second, simply to assimilate them through the routes that other people get them by, but to *retain* them. I am rather for the latter course, though I would not be completely averse to mixing in a little of the former as well. But I think that with a fairly steady reading of newspapers, popular newsmagazines like *Time* and *Newsweek*, and other sources of this sort the technical vocabulary, which is marvelously wonderful and exciting to me, can be had in its larger aspects. The question then becomes how and where to avail oneself of the more specialized vocabulary that does not get into *Time* and *Newsweek*. This will bear a good deal of pondering, I think.

I am now going over a very large work on the painting and sculpture of Ben Nicholson. He is the *kind* of artist that I have never been able to like very much, not having built into my personality and not being able to acquire, either, the response to his extremely rarefied and simplified kinds of constructs. He is almost too pure to believe; all those rectangles, all those chaste circles, all those lines so mercilessly in harmony with each other. And yet I enjoy Nicholson very much. *That* kind of purity must be paid attention to. Surely this is so. I notice, in the introduction to this Abrams volume, that John Russell says, "Even the most apparently severe of his works turns out to be made up of innumerable decisions small and large, in which the hand was as important as the brain." That is an interesting notion as to how the artist works. Surely there are analogies in poetry. The "hand" in poetry is not doing exactly what the hand in painting or sculpture is doing, of course, but there is an analogy just the same. I am not quite sure what, in poetry, corresponds to the hand, but there surely *is* something. There is a dual thing working here, just as certainly as there is in molding clay, laying on color, or carving with a knife or other implement. There *is* a sense in which language is *material*, and this must be paid attention to, utilized, and finally transformed.

I have started a new book of poetry and have three poems in it so far. These have all been sent off to *The New Yorker*, and I am awaiting words. Meanwhile, what to turn to? Which poem shall I work on next? I think I

shall work on "The Rain Guitar" and "Three Poems of
Flight Sleep." I have literally hundreds waiting in the
wings, but those three seem to be to me the most
promising subjects I have. I also want to do some
experimental writing, along lines which I have never
before explored. What these lines will be I have no idea
at all, but only the hint of a couple of directions. This
is the most exciting to me of all my projects. I know I
can write the poems of flight sleep and others of that
sort, which are mainly anecdotal, as is most of my work
to date. But I want now to move into something more
timeless, less narrative-oriented, and altogether different.
I will be very pure about these poems, hoping that in
the end they will cross-fertilize with the other things that
I am writing and produce a style that none of us could
have foreseen.

What to do about next summer? If we do all go to
Europe, what attitude should I take toward the trip? That
is, how can I really *give* Europe to my brother and his
wife, to say nothing of to Maxine and Kevin? For
example, what emphasis should I put on the *history* of
the places we go to? This can be fascinating to some
people, and boring in the extreme to others. I think Patsy
would be very much interested in the history of the
places that we visit, all of them perhaps, or surely some
of them. On the other hand, Tom would not. He is
fascinated by the American Civil War and by little else.
Am I assuming too much in hoping that he will read
up a bit on the history of Europe, and so consequently
derive more benefit and pleasure from the trip? I don't
know. I rather doubt that he will. I have really very little
notion of what he would enjoy about Europe, beyond
some of the scenery, some of the people, and some of
the food. I am quite sure he would enjoy the boat trip,
and maybe some of London, a little of Paris, and a little
of Italy. But he surely would *not* like the museums or

any of the things that Patsy would quickly become
rapturous about. Like all European trips, I guess, this one
is going to have to be a compromise in which one does
something he doesn't much want to do and that someone
else *does* want to do, in order to be able to do something
of what he wants to do that someone else does not
particularly want to do.

In *Death's Baby Machine* there is a scene toward the
beginning where the protagonist, Cahill, sits in his
office at the swimming pool. He has had a one-way
mirror put in between the girls' dressing room and his
office, and it pleases him to sit there and wonder who
will come in and dress and undress, with the emphasis
on the undressing, in front of him, not knowing he is
there. He could easily have had all the booths done in
these mirrors, but the game-interest of the situation
pleases him, and he enjoys things better that way.
There is this sense of someone coming into his power,
part of the power being based on chance. This could
be quite a good scene, and could be quite revelatory of
Cahill's temperament, including some of things about it
that he himself is not completely aware of.

In "The Indian Maiden" it might be possible to have the
narrator quite literally blow up, and free-associate for
a couple of pages. This might be magnificent; it might
be ridiculous. Anyway, try it.

Matthew Bruccoli wants me to edit a volume of essays
on my own work, to be sponsored by the Merrill
Foundation. I am to talk to him tomorrow at lunch
about this. If I decided to do it, what would I use?
The Leiberman essay, surely, the Weatherby essay,
perhaps the two Bly essays, pro and con, the
Untermeyer essay, maybe one or two by R. W. Flint,
the one by Charles Monaghan, perhaps one or two

student thesis, and so on. I have two sources of essays:
these are the clippings and magazines that I have saved,
and the Glancy bibliography. I will surely want to
include Peter Davison's essay on Robert Lowell and
myself, and there are a good many others to choose
from. If this book is going to appear, that will mean
that I have five volumes coming out within the next
year. That is a lot.

I am now in the place in the biography of Hart Crane
where his worst and final years are upon him. The
amount of alcohol he drinks is absolutely staggering,
especially in Mexico, and I am surprised he did not die,
as Dylan Thomas did, of a "massive insult to the brain."
I am awed by all this drinking of Crane's; it seems
superhuman in some ways. I have always felt that I
could drink with most men, but I could not stay with
Hart Crane's alcoholic consumption for half an hour,
much less the days on end he kept it up. That kind of
thing is beyond or outside my temperament. I can drink
probably more than most people, and probably do, but
I am not really a very good madman. I guess I will last
longer that way. Or I hope so, at any rate.

There has never been in the history of the world and
never will be anyone whom the wilderness fascinates as
much as it does me. I don't know the wilderness well,
the woods or the mountains, but the wilderness,
anywhere it can be found, is a subject of endless
interest and rejoicing to me. It is because it is so strange
to me and so utterly foreign to anything that I have
known that I do not really wish to become any better
acquainted with the wilderness *technically* than I already
am: only enough to survive whatever situations I might
encounter. But who knows what those might be? Most
of my poems about woods and lakes and rivers and so
on depend on my *not* knowing these things very well,

so that they remain strange to me: that is, so that they remain in at least some sense *visions*. I remember when I was hunting with Chris and Lewis King a few years ago, I went off the road about half a mile by myself to hunt. I quickly became lost and turned to go in the direction that I thought the road lay in. It was not there, and I came over a little rise and looked down into a valley with a creek in it that I had never laid eyes on. Before terror hit me, I thought I was in Heaven: completely lost, completely in wonder.

I don't know why this recollection keeps returning to me as one of the saddest things I have ever had in my mind. It is something I merely read in a newspaper, concerning a location in Vietnam where American troops were bivouacked. A tiger came out of the jungle during the night and tried to seize one of the soldiers, and he leapt up, grabbed his submachine gun, the other soldiers grabbed their weapons—rifles, machine guns, grenades— and all turned on the tiger and blew and shot him almost into nothingness. Why is this so sad? But it is; it is.

Miserable day at the range yesterday. I was almost 100 points below the scores that I have been shooting lately. This inconsistency is the worst thing about my archery, and comes, I am quite sure, from the fact that I am of an extremely nervous and explosive temperament, and standing still and being calm about things and doing them in a routine manner, as one must do in archery, is as unnatural to me as anything could possibly be. And yet the fact that I have shot scores up to 430 indicates that I *can* shoot well; the point is to find a way to enable myself to do so consistently. The trouble is with my release: there is that hysteria. I do not seem able to get a consistently relaxed release, and when the right hand snaps open something also happens to the left hand: I throw the bow either to the left or the right or up. All this can be taken care of with a lot of practice and concentration.

I shot both the Hoyt and the Howatt bows yesterday, and I have changed my mind. The Howatt is a little easier to pull back, though both bows are of exactly the same weight, and it seems to *sling* the arrow rather than snap it out. It is the snap in the Hoyt bow that gave me the illusion that it is the faster bow, when in fact they are almost exactly the same, with the Howatt perhaps a shade faster, in fact. I think with the easier draw plus the enormously massive and heavy handle section, that will give me a little extra shooting edge over the Hoyt. But they are both very good bows indeed, and I am very lucky to have them. Now we must do something about the man behind the bow, whichever one he may finally settle upon.

This kind of relaxed rhythm I am pursuing in poetry needs to be altered by quite another kind of thing. I don't know exactly what I want yet, but it will be something altogether harsher. I want something jolting and rocky-mouthed; something abrasive and sudden and jolting, and altogether imaginative. Let us work something out on these terms, if we can find the way to do it.

In the new novel the son is both the best cadet—at least in the air—and the worst on the ground. There is some hint that he does this deliberately: that is, he demonstrates his superiority and then disdains the system publicly. There also should be some indication that the post commandant cannot get rid of his best flying cadet of that class, otherwise the other cadets will give him trouble and maybe even mutiny, or at least raise hell in a number of ways. This would provide a kind of motivation for the boy's murder. Or so it seems to the father, if to no one else. Joel Cahill must be seen as in some ways the precursor of the current protesting kids.

The difference is that he believes that an effective protest must be made by one who has conquered the system and then repudiated it. He believes that his excellence in the air constitutes mastery of the system, which he can then denounce from that position. I think this is valid psychologically as well as socially, and we must make this apparent without being obvious.

Also in the new novel, the long conversation between father and the cadet who is caught "in the machine." It is literally the "washing machine," the bureaucratic organization that eases the unworthy cadet out of the program. All this is discussed, and the name of Joel Cahill is brought into the conversation, perhaps, without the boy's knowing that Cahill is Joel's father. This might be a very good conversation, a good dialogue making plain a good deal of the Air Force's policies, and the growing mysteriousness of Joel. The machine also could be taken as the gigantic bureaucracy of the Air Force, and, by extension, of the machine bureaucracies against which the kids of today are revolting. Once in the machine, there is nothing for it but to be crushed by it. Once started downhill a cadet or any other person in the machine is doomed to be discarded by it. In some ways this is necessary: we are, after all, "fighting a war." But the implications of the machine are far more sinister than this, and we should show them as such.

The Machine is a fairly interesting title because it does not apply to any real machine, except perhaps the aircraft the boys are flying, and those they will fly later. The machine, however, that I am really referring to is the bureaucratic machine of the Air Force, and the social system that makes it possible and even mandatory. It is a thing which human beings must go through, be rejected by, or survive, but can never really escape from.

As to style. I must take whatever I can from the
enormously complicated and convoluted novelistic work
of James Gould Cozzen's *Guard of Honor*, which gives
the best sense of military bureaucracy that I know,
especially as it applies to the organization of the Air
Force. This, together with what I remember from
experience, should do *that* part of it. Walker Percy's style
in *The Last Gentleman* should give some hints also. But
really I am after something completely different from
either of these writers. The style must be much different
from Cozzen's and Percy's, and also different from that
of *Deliverance*. This is perhaps the hardest part of the
whole enterprise.

Could there possibly be in the novel a brief excerpt of
a home movie or flickering Air Force movie which shows
the cadets at a parade or even on the flight line, and
a brief stop action of Joel? This might be very effective.
Think about it. It could be shown Cahill by the public
relations officer or even by the commandant himself, but
told to him as it appears.

If we show the movie, then Joel can be seen briefly
glancing back over his shoulder, and it might be
explained to Cahill that where he is looking with a
mixture of anger and some nameless other emotion is
toward the commandant's AT-6, though the aircraft
itself might not be shown in the actual picture.

What I want from the guitar is a combination of
precision—that is *clean*ness—and abandon. Also a very
great degree of relaxation in both hands, particularly the
right.

Write to Wallace Stegner at Stanford and give him a vote
of confidence on his stand on conservation. Also say
something about his novels, which I have always enjoyed

enormously, and about his story "Field Guide to the
Western Birds," which I think is one of the best I've
ever read. See if you can get him to send you his last
book, or at least give you the name of it, so that you can
read it. This is a good man, much maligned simply
because he is the head of a creative writing program.
I remember seeing him on television, and he seemed to
me extremely fuzzy-minded and unhelpful to the
young writer with whom he was working. I think that
Stegner's main value will be in his own works, though he
has undoubtedly done some good things at Stanford.

The example of Pound's cantos: that a great scholar, or
a hit-or-miss scholar, can bring together a diverse number
of subjects, and the details of these subjects, and present
them as a poem, points up a peculiarity of modern
poetry, which is this: that if one is persuaded by
whatever means—the press, the critics, friends—that a
man is a great poet, there will follow a large number of
commentators who will take the writer's vagaries as
gospel, and will spend their lives running them down,
explicating them, and justifying them. Surely this is a
very curious situation, and not without its comical aspect.

Diction. "Flight burns." Things happen that really do not
happen in the world. Think some things through on this
basis.

Have been reading essays: the new one by Howard Moss
and several by Gore Vidal. Moss's are literary, and Vidal's
are literary and cultural. Vidal is quite a good critic,
I think. He has a very urbane, civilized, and rather
worldly intelligent view that is very much the view of
an in-group mentality. He is quite outspoken in his
opinions, none of which are fashionable outside a small
similarly minded group of literati. Howard Moss is very
good also: very acute on the few writers he likes and

has written about. But his essays do not have the bite of Vidal's. The question is, is bite all that necessary? Vidal seems to think it is, and so do a good many others. I am not at all sure.

I do not wish to say anything in poetry *neatly*. That is the main trouble with Dick Wilbur's poetry: the sense of habitual dispatch. This is not only, in the end, tiresome, but even comes to seem a kind of poetical reflex. That is the wrong way to get a poem to behave.

I suppose that one of the things I have always disliked about poetry is that when you read most poems, the first line already announces itself as "poetry." There is something about a special kind of poetry-language which I have always disliked very much. One of the things I wanted to do several years ago was to make a poetry that would not seem like poetry, or at least like the other poetry around. To a certain extent I have done this, but I wish to do something else now. What?

Remark of James Feibleman in Martha's Vineyard last summer: "I have always wanted to write philosophy." This is curious. Does one "write" philosophy in the sense that one writes novels and poetry and plays? I have never heard of the production of philosophical works referred to in this way.

Have just finished reading Ralph Vaughan Williams' book of essays, *National Music*. The story of Williams' musical education is quite interesting. The formal quality of the education of a composer is basically different from the rather hit-or-miss ways in which writers become writers. One studies to be a composer in some sense as one studies to be a doctor; there doesn't seem to be any other way. Someone once remarked that there was no composer of note who had not gone to a conservatory.

Is this true? I don't know, but I imagine it is. Compared to the composition of symphonies and concertos, I should think that the composition of a book of poetry would be relatively easy. But then, I am inevitably thrown off the track of the truth because writing poetry to *me* is easy, while I could not write a musical composition of even the slightest interest. There is a case for innate ability, talent, or genius. I don't think these things will ever be understood, nor should they be.

Passage in a book by Harry Levin on Christopher Marlowe: "With him we not only taste the alluring fruit; we walk in the sunlit innocence of the garden; and, plunging back farther into primordial darkness, we seem to witness the blinding flash of creation."

Write to John Lehmann about his recent book *In My Own Time*. I have the previous parts of this, and they have always seemed to me to be balanced, informative, and, in the end, moving books. Maybe it's just that I like books like this; but if that is true, and it is, it also means I have read a great many *of* such books. Judging from this condition, I can truthfully say that *In My Own Time* is very likely a masterpiece. Lehmann is no great literary genius—his poems are respectable enough, but hardly exciting—but he has *been* there: he has lived the history of his time as an intellectual in England during the war, and before and after, and has put it down. People should read what he has recorded.

There is a kind of truism among poets and literary critics and people interested in these matters generally, that the poet is someone who lives more intensely, responds more manically, and in general *exists* more than other people. But this business of a cultivated—as I am convinced most of it is—overresponsiveness does not lead at all to the kind of angelic being that the poet is supposed to have.

In fact it leads to the individual's decline, and often in a very rapid fashion. He becomes, in fact, a mess. What happens to him is usually a mental disorder of some kind, or, as in the case of Hart Crane and Dylan Thomas, suicide of one sort or the other. What is needed is a sense of measure of some sort: Montherlant's theory of *alternance*.

And how, come to think of it, should such an absolute bastard as Montherlant have so much accurate observation about human life and human behavior? He is a person I cannot abide, and in many ways he is very much like me. Not exactly, but very much, in his outlook and approach to existence. Or, rather, I'm like him.

The terror of middle age is like the terror of George Orwell's beggar in the streets of a large city: people look at you but they do not notice you. In some ways you have already become a ghost. The most awful thing about middle age is that you are simply a body with nothing particular to recommend it. Who wants to see a middle-aged man standing around, for example, at a public crowd, such as appears at a football game? Most of the young people are nondescript enough, but a middle-aged man—or woman—is nondescriptness itself. There is only a body waiting to fill a grave. There proceeds from this the terrible kind of sheepishness of middle-aged people: the self-effacing quality, or, even more terrible, the kind of assertiveness that many of them have. They feel that, well, we've come along this far and people God damn well *ought* to pay attention to us because we have, haven't we, acquired a good deal of wisdom, or at least some. This is rarely the case. The only *raison d'être* for being middle-aged or old is the possession of an absolute mastery of *something*. Otherwise the aging process is a ridiculous spectacle, and sadder than anyone could possibly believe, did it not appear to all of us every day of our lives.

The title of the new book of poems is now *Slowly Toward Hercules*. Let us really do something with space, with the galaxies, with the evolutionary trend of the universe. This is tremendously important, and with your background in astronomy, which in some sense can be picked up again, this may provide an interesting and maybe vital direction. Start reading.

In poetry, one sickens of art-language.

To lay down that situation which *must* involve the reader in an action: that is what I want my poems to do. Many poems are incapable of *involving* the reader, but just go on and rehearse a scene or action that in itself has little vitality or little interest. I want my poem to *devour* the reader, so that he cannot possibly put it down as he reads it, or forget about it when he finishes.

I wish the poem to be a large, intense and *complete* experience.

Making some progress on languages; a few words a day. But if you keep putting these into practice and reading things all the time, it is amazing how quickly things fall into place. The trouble with all languages is verbs. That, and idiomatic usages. One never gets these last completely straight, for they keep changing. But most of the main ones you can obtain, use, and understand.

"Swarm" is a good word. So is "flock." Why?

In "The Bridge" Crane had the problem of approximating a kind of narrative structure using the language of bedazzlement that he had invented. Did he do this? No; not very well. But it can be done; narrative can sustain this, though the connotative language must be a radically different sort from Crane's. Let us try a kind of connotative language, first on still objects or scenes, and then on moving ones. This will take some time, but it should be enormously interesting even so. Is not experimentation what we live for?

That strange, strange lucidity: that is the thing I want. The poem should be as though the most astonishing things were being said in a radically new and simple kind of English. It should be as though the reader had turned a corner of the English language and come upon an entirely new and infinitely more imaginative way to use it.

In most of my poems I want a sense of *story*. There are two ways to do this, basically. One way is for the story to be obvious; that is, for there to be a beginning, middle, and end in that order. The other way is for the story to be implicit, and there are a million ways of doing this. Both methods are good, though the latter way offers more of a challenge, and is probably of more value than the other, at least for me.

Read part of a review in *The Hudson Review* by William Dickey which dealt with Anne Sexton. He has isolated, exactly, the quality in her work that I have always detested, which is its self-indulgence. This, I guess, is part of what I meant by "suspect" in poetry. I surely ought to write William Dickey and tell him what a valuable critical term I believe this to be. I wonder if he is still at San Francisco State?

The guitar takes up a lot of my time, but it seems pure, innocent pleasure to me. I started too late ever to play like Merle Travis or Chet Atkins—no, surely *that* is out of sight. But neither will the instrument ever be a source of *income* to me; that is, drudgery. It will never consume my whole life and my whole being, but remain a pleasure.

After almost seven years, I can play better than most of the college boys I run into, and a whole lot better than any high school boy I have ever come upon. Perhaps it is absurd to take a certain amount of pleasure in such things, but I do. And indeed, why not?

In the new novel, it is important that Cahill has never flown before; he has never been off the ground. In this way, I can suggest some of this sense of the *miraculousness* of flight. There is only one flight in the book, and this is at dusk, when Joel's instructor flies Cahill back from the auxiliary field to the main field in a Stearman. This should last fifteen or twenty pages, and they should be awfully good pages.

As it looks now, the novel will run about 300 pages or 350. There must be more interaction between people in this book, and a good many more scenes than there are in *Deliverance*.

In the new book, we should also attempt to do something with the athletic setup at the base: the football, the basketball, the physical training tests, the long runs in formation, and so on. There also might be a small section here where the instructors, all of whom except the check-riders are civilians, play football with the cadets. Cahill might also play, for a down or two. Think this out; it may yield something rather good.

For a poem to build well: to proceed at the proper speed and weight, and to come up, inexorably, to a point higher than the one it started with, and then to resolve things there in an unforgettable manner: well, one wishes for that.

And yet, with this sense of building, the poet also has an additional monkey on his back, which is that when the reader is brought up to this eminence, he will not be satisfied with anything less than a crashing kind of conclusion that leaves him limp. And that is a pretty hard job for the poor poet to have to attend to. Nevertheless, that is what he should be doing, or trying to do.

The trouble with so much poetry one reads nowadays, that makes one book so much like the next, is that the lines and the poems have no rhythmic thrust. They are flat and non-committal and rather complacent, especially the stuff by the women, which all sounds as though it were written by the same rather synthetic, flat-speaking, neurotic, and quietly desperate person. This is awfully tiresome to me. One can catalogue at least ten or twenty names of these poets, and, though one may admit that they have all collectively found a kind of style, one is saddened that it is so prevalent that no woman poet can write any other way. Sad, indeed.

The most important single ingredient that any poem can have is a sense of *necessity*. There must be this sense of urgency and consequence, all in an imaginative kind of communication. The poem can have this impetus of rhythm and urgency either obviously, as in Hopkins, or quietly, as in Supervielle. But it has to be there for the poem to have the kind of chance of being memorable in the reader's mind that it should have. I must spend the rest of my life finding out ways to get this quality down on paper.

The one quality in poetry that I am coming more and more to dislike is the offhand. Elizabeth Bishop is the chief sinner in this regard; consequently, I simply cannot read anything she writes. I have always believed very much in convincingness of tone, but Miss Bishop's kind of offhandness is, in fact, more studied than all the rhetorical devices of Gerard Manley Hopkins, or even John Berryman.

There are several poets I have been wrong about, and as
wrong as it is possible to be wrong. One of these is
John Berryman. I pick up one of his books now and look
at it, and I am simply appalled at what I see. He is the
epitome of all those poets who, though naturally of
uninteresting and academic minds, wish to make
themselves appear to be interesting and, in some cases,
like Berryman's, wild men. Berryman is a timid little
academic who stays drunk all the time—it is easy to do
—in order to convince himself and others that he is
inhabited by the true demon, such as Rimbaud or Dylan
Thomas was. In keeping with this, he tortures his poems
up, deliberately misspells words, wrenches the syntax
around in various ways that are easy enough to do, if
one sets one's mind to it, in order to make "an original"
poetry. Some of it has a certain doctored-up intensity, but
it is all so phony and ersatz that I for one have less and
less and less interest in it. Berryman has painted himself
into a corner, and I shall not go in there to get those
few good moments that all this artificiality turns up.
When I read *Bradstreet* I thought maybe this was a new
way for American poetry. I do not think so anymore.
Poetry has got to be less artificial and more convincing
as speech than Berryman is ever likely to become. That
is beyond him; he has walled himself off with artifice,
and will stay there until he and his work die.

Many chord studies on guitar. These are very valuable.
The whole instrument is opening up in ways I never
thought possible. Tremendous fascination of combinations
of sound. One simply cannot get enough of them. The
possibilities for musical expressiveness are endless: the
permutations and combinations are absolutely amazing and
endlessly fascinating.

Poets like Anne Sexton, Ann Stevenson, Adrienne Rich,
and others have a rather studied way of avoiding any

kind of rhetorical statement. They want to be discovered
by the reader saying something quirky and offhand. But
any kind of grandeur of statement is never going to be
made in that way. Anyone who courts sublimity has to
run the risk of looking ridiculous, and that is the one
thing that these poets will not do. They are desperately
afraid of being caught out; of being rhetorical or
bombastic. But the way to glory of statement has run
this particular hazard. There is no other way.

The longer I live, the longer and better the whole
perspective of possibility becomes, and the more I see
how necessary it is to *throw* one's self open to the least
chance impulse or stimulus coming from anywhere. Who
knows where that "anywhere" comes from, or is? It can
be the slightest thing, it can be something immortal in
literature or art, it can be the way a high jumper takes off
his warm-up pants. No wonder Whitman is the poet who
opened up America for us: he was open to *all* kinds of
possibilities. A man sawing a plank was a great man to
Whitman and imminently worth watching and learning
from.

It is the entrance of the glib that one must stand most
rigorous watch against. Glibness is the thing that destroys
most poets, when they are poets to be destroyed. Glibness
is the ease of statement of the moment, whether this ease
has to do with suffering, with patriotism, with sex, or
with anything else. Glibness is glibness in any generation.

I can remember those marvelous days when I would
prowl through one library after another: the Fresno
County Free Library, for example, where I sat reading
Faulkner's *Light in August* with some sense of a
revelation which never came, or the Atlanta Public
Library when I came back from the war, and stole a few
books which I still have now, giving way to the touch,

flaking into anonymity. It is a certain shock to me to
realize that it is now the younger fellows who are
prowling through libraries and perhaps stealing my books.
Can it possibly be that someone thinks of me as the
answer to everything?

It might be possible to send a kind of psychic message
to Eugene McCarthy from a long-forgotten manifesto of
literature in the thirties. This is from C. Day Lewis' essay
of many years ago, *Revolution in Literature:* "We see in
this a warning that no social group built around an
individual can succeed today. The pressure of world
events, bearing so heavily upon it, will sooner or later
prove too much for the central individual, and thus
explode the small group."

It seems to me that I am the bearer of some kind of
immortal message to humankind. What is this message?
I don't know, but it exists.

As a kind of man of letters, I look at the English
literary scene. Seldom have I noticed so many brilliant
men, so many good poets, so many ready polemicists. And
yet what is the issue of this? Because England is failing,
her poets, brilliant as they are, seem hangdog and sad.
There is no escape from influence and power. England
might produce a magnificent poet as she goes down, but
he will henceforth be known as the-poet-who-came-into-
his-genius-when-England-went-down. There is no help for
this; it is simply the way of the world. The main thing
is not to be on the losing team.

Tried once more to read the poetry of John Lehmann.
Never have I so desperately wished to like the writings
of a poet. But the stuff is absolutely and irrevocably
mediocre. It is not only mediocre; it is less good, even,
than that. How is it possible for a man to have lived

through what Lehmann has lived through and not come up with anything more compelling than the rather tame verses that are all he has to show from the years of the London blitz, and those before that, and those after? Why is there no *monstrousness* in the man? Why is he so even-tempered and nice about everything? He has been through enough to drive a regiment of soldiers berserk. And yet he maintains the even tenor of his ways, recording who his friends are and what he published in his magazines and his book-publishing ventures. His world, the world of the Battle of Britain, demands a tongue of fire to tell what *could* be told. And yet John Lehmann sits calmly back and is nice and judicious and friendly about it all. Why?

There are really only two kinds of poets: those who generalize and those who describe states of being.

The sadness of middle age is absolutely unfathomable; there is no bottom to it. Everything you do is sad. If you look at a football game, you are only a middle-aged man looking at a football game. If you eat a sandwich in a public place, it is sadness beyond any ever conceived of in the Lamentations of the Old Testament. And if you look at a girl on the street, she makes it a point not to look back, and that is sadness also. The only possibility lies in the past: if you are middle-aged, and aging, then your strength lies in what those years have given you. The only excuse for old age is mastery, and this depends on many years of devotion to the thing that you have mastered. But without mastery, middle age is a joke and old age is Hell itself, the inferno.

I think with terrible sadness of the evening spent with the astronauts a couple of nights before Walter Schirra's lift-off. I was drunk out of my mind, and

could not focus on anything that happened, but simply
sat in a corner in a drunken stupor attempting
conversation with one or another nice young fellow
who drifted by, doubtless out of a sense of duty, or of
some kind of obscure loyalty to the *Life* people
I was with. That opportunity will not come to me
again, that is certain. And yet if I had been cold sober,
what would I have done? Would I have been an
eager-eyed middle-aged fellow, terribly receptive to all
their personalities, and so on? No; if I had it to do
again, I would be a drunken poet among the astronauts.
And, by God, I was a drunken poet. I remember them;
now let them remember me.

Mediocre day at the range today. But I *can* shoot well.
It is all a matter of concentration, and of *willing* the
body into a state of relaxation, from which the arrow
leaps. It is all so amazingly easy when one does what
one should do.

I am sick of poets who tell us, in a clever and/or
sensitive way, what we all know. I want now to gear
myself up to say what nobody could have thought of in
a hundred million years. This is coming; I feel it.

All these poets who find their whole careers in telling
you, better than you could tell it, your own reality.
But I want to make a new reality; this one is not
good enough. Words can change it all, if they come
from the right direction and fall on the right ears.

Quoting Day Lewis, in speaking of William Faulkner
". . . who can create that kind of supernatural tension
amid commonplace events which is the sign of epic."

So many poems; so many poets: the reason people are
not interested in reading them is that they *do* nothing

very interesting. One is prepared to hear Anne Sexton
bitch about her menstruation problems only just so
long, even if one is a woman. The trouble is that the
personalities of these poets, and these protagonists,
is so irrevocably commonplace. The poets who write
out of such convictions as this are convinced that their
rapport is the source of their strength: that is, their
rapport with the rest of humanity in these native
ills. This is not true, however. The reader, and the
human being, demands, really, something more
extraordinary than this: something dramatic, strange,
crazy, memorable.

Verbal *velocity*.

The pattern of a life: nothing is more important.
I lie here reading Cecil Day Lewis' early revolutionary
statements and poems, which appeared when I was in
the seventh grade. Day Lewis is now Poet Laureate.
He and I had a very pleasant exchange of telegrams
a couple of years ago. What has happened here? Perhaps
what should have happened; perhaps not. But the life
of Day Lewis is gone now. What should he have done?
What could he have done?

How sad it all is, this trying to be Immortal, this
desperate attempt to say something memorable. But I,
like Yeats, would cast all that out. If I did not believe
that the whole literary effort was a hell of a lot of
fun—exciting, perhaps superhuman fun—I would not
do it. I had rather go for some big archery trophy,
and spend my time practicing my release.

There is a time in the aging process when a terrible,
reverse miracle seems to have happened. You see people
that you know from day to day, and they scarcely
seem older at all. But you have an image of people

in your mind, and if you are removed from them for a certain period—say a couple of years, a number of years—*then* see them, an extremely awful, even metaphysical change seems to have taken place in them. You look at them, and you can scarcely recognize them. Nor they you.

Always distrust writers who insist on using their middle names. In a woman it is understandable, though not likable. In a man it is inexcusable.

The awful thing about growing older is that one can feel one's sense of the consequence of things—the *feeling* of their consequence—leaking away day by day. No matter what situation one finds oneself in, it is always the same; the main sentiment that occurs to one is simply "what does it matter?" In middle age, with the end probably still a good ways off, but maybe not, one is resigned in the most terrible way. The list of the possibilities of the things that one can do grows shorter and shorter. But much more terrible than that is the fact that the list of things that one *wants* to do gets shorter and shorter, faster and faster.

Someone said of my poetry that it attempts to win back for poetry some of the territory that poetry has unnecessarily relinquished to the novel. That is accurate. I like very much the emphasis on narrative that this implies, but above all the emphasis on *action* of some kind. If one describes in a poem the wheels-up landing of an aircraft, this might be said to be borrowed from novelistic technique. But for it to be poetry the words must be much better chosen, and the rhythm and the *drive* of the words must be much more telling. It is prose, if you will, but raised to the height of poetry, which is what poetry always was, anyway.

In other words, in keeping with the last entry, I
want, more than anything else, for the poem to be an
experience—that is, a *physical* experience—for the reader.
It must be a completed action, and the plunging in of the
reader into this action is the most difficult and the most
desirable feat that the poet can perform. Nothing can be
more important than this: it is the difference between
poetry of reflection and poetry of participation. I go
all-out for participation. It may not restore the soul, but it
restores the body.

Coinage of new words: "swaysift," for dust in water,
seen in a ray of light. This could be very exciting:
coinages after the German, and those original with me.

In the entry a couple of entries ago, I spoke of the
restoration of the body. After all, the body is nothing
less or more than the sense of being of a particular
creature at a particular time and place. Everything he
perceives and thinks depends upon his bodily state.
Stanley Burnshaw shows this beautifully in *The
Seamless Web*.

I want a fever, in poetry: a fever, and tranquillity.

Weidlé says: "It is easier to eliminate *a* form, than
form."

Kind of poetic figure: the thing against itself, or a
variety of itself: wind against wind, sea against sea,
fire against fire.

Another type of poetic figure: joining or connecting:
I join your shadow to the water, I connect you to the
bums underground.

The phrase woman-light.

Beauty, as in the case of a woman's beauty, is a dead end. Ultimately, it is self-defeating.

All this riot business, all this student take-over business: maybe this will blast some of this overrefinement out of us. But we'll get it back again; intelligence always leads to overrefinement: to its own overrefinement. Susan Sontag will be right back, talking about simplicity.

Why do I so consciously avoid Southern novels about families? I don't know; I don't believe it's a question of my overfamiliarity with the subject at all. But these are among the most boring of all novels to me, no matter how subtly refined they are, or how true to life. Whenever I see one in a bookstore, I go right on by. And I'm sure this will be true for me for the rest of my life.

What writers simply cannot understand is that overrefinement of the sensibility leads the animal man off into sterility and inconsequentiality. What one needs are large, basic emotions, and not endlessly subtle talk, palaver, and analysis.

It is good for a poet to remember that the human mind, though in some ways quite complicated, is in some others very simple. It can only hold one image at a time, though one cannot say quite how long this time lasts. But for a given time—let us say a short time—it can contemplate only one thing that is given it. It is good to remember this, and to utilize it.

What is it I see in the writings of Ronald Firbank? He is more like a put-on than a real writer—except that he *is* a real writer, and says some things, almost on every page, that are absolutely marvelous. His put-onness is not nearly as charming to me as it is to people like Auden,

but in the occasional phrase he is marvelous. Witness, in
Valmouth, the statement of the story's central lady, who,
wishing to be memorialized in the stained-glass window of
a church, says that she wishes to be surrounded by a
"brutality of stone."

How on earth can such a learned man as C. S. Lewis
write such trite poetry? It seems as though this would be
impossible, but when the page opens, there it is.

This fanatical ambition to compose long "masterpieces"
in prose—or even in verse—has never been at all
attractive to me. It is a sad fact—sad, so to say, for the
novelists—that all their enormous brickwork or marble
edifices are in most cases less memorable than a single line.
Poetry is inevitably going to have the last say. The line is
there, and the memorability, and the thing that can change
your life, if this is indeed possible in words at all.

In poetry, is there any way out of the narrative? Should
there be? The narrative element, the poem with a definite
beginning, a definite middle, and a definite end, the thrust
through time, has always been of immense importance in
almost everything I have written. Should I look for ways
to vary the narrative, or try to conceive new subjects, or
new methods of treating them? What, exactly? There
ought to be some new way to get the sense of narrative
thrust without using the conventional ways of portraying
narrative. Another possibility is the perfectly static poem:
the purely presentational poem, though with infinite depth
and strangeness.

Why this longing for new people? Ah, that can never be
understood, or relieved. It is beyond belief, and stronger
than anything else in life: this intolerable longing for
something unknown that comes to one in the center of
one's comfort.

In sexual experience, one has the answer to a very great deal of human anxiety and uncertainty. For one thing, sex *is* certain: it is a quick clean and total release, and as therapy for a very great many human conditions, it has the utmost possible importance. There is no mystery in this, and I see no reason for the complicating of the essentially very clear issue that goes on in all minds: of psychoanalysts, of commentators on sex of any and all kinds. The thing itself is so basic that all these intellectualizations about it and around it seem laughable, and do the marvelous, primitive cleansing action of the thing a great deal of disservice.

Horace Gregory has got me interested in Dorothy Richardson. I should now like to get hold of *Pilgrimage* and read it, plus whatever letters and journals of hers the Gotham Book Mart can turn up for me. Inquire within the next couple of days.

I love the long, long discipline which pays off slowly but fully, if one has been devoted long enough. A lot of people would say that I put too much time in on the guitar, and I occasionally think so too. But when I pick it up now, after seven years of finger-picking, I know that I can do what I can do. I know that every move of my fingers has been paid for by dozens of hours of playing, and this gives me intense satisfaction. This is why I like so much Mississippi John Hurt's explanation of why he was not nervous at his first public concert, after having played for so many years to nothing but field hands. Ralph Rinzler or some city sophisticate asked Mississippi John why he was not nervous, and John said: "Because I knows what I knows. I knows it, and I *been* knowing it."

There is a term called gallows humor. Somebody ought to invent a term called gallows cuteness, and apply it to the work of Sylvia Plath, Anne Sexton, and the others like them. This is a special kind of predictable ghastly, self-satisfied, and complacent joking about matters like death, disease, and so on. There can be no greater falsification than this; it is literature, it is the *literary*, at its worst.

Win Scott says that the only way to be a genius is to be born one. Not so. Genius is the discovery of an idiom. It is the discovery of an idiom, the successful exploration and exploitation of it, and the extensive employment of it. It is something discovered, not innate.

Read a lot more philosophy, particularly contemporary philosophy. What on earth are those fellows *doing?*

Emil Oppfer, who lived with Hart Crane at 110 Columbia Heights, where Crane did some of his greatest writing and conceiving, told John Unterecker that there was "nothing dirty" in their relationship. One wonders what Oppfer's definition of "dirty" is. Nevertheless, he is right, no matter what he means.

Who killed Sharon Tate? I didn't.

I would like it said of me that I had a muscular sensibility.

The best of all wives is the country girl, and the next best is the prostitute who manages to get married, and who must work hard all the rest of her life at recovering the love and the sensuality that she spent a number of years losing for money.

Someone has been practicing scales and exercises on the guitar year after year, for years. When *he* rips loose with the thing, it matters. He *can* rip. Thus, the true meaning of spontaneity.

Happened to read, in the letters column of a long-forgotten issue of *Playboy*, a despairing cry from a young fellow in Florida who was going bald at twenty-two, and asking *Playboy* for advice. *Playboy* replied something to the effect that he should cultivate his body, "get a terrific build," or become "interesting" and "a lot of fun" in other ways. *Playboy* assured him that appearances were *really* not everything. This very sage advice from a magazine in which appearances are not only a great deal, but are, quite literally, all there is!

There is always this thing in me between doing the thing of the maximum physical pleasure and that of the maximum physical difficulty, toughness. How long will I hang between these two? For the rest of my life probably, or for as long as I hold out.

But one thing is certain: that is, that when the toughness, when the self-discipline goes, so do I.

I am quite convinced that the secret of a long-term successful relationship with another person is the ability to put up with the other person's mannerisms. There are certain things that certain people do, and do all the time, that simply drive you up the wall. I am sure that incompatible mannerisms have broken up more marriages than sex troubles, money troubles, or all other kinds of usually stated grounds. Really, the only true ground for the dissolution of a marriage is mannerism.

I don't believe that people who are not themselves creative artists ever can really know how physically exhausting it is to write poetry, or paint, or compose music. In my own case, I seem to be in a good period of my creative life now, and the reason I know this is that I am physically so exhausted every night that I can hardly get into bed. What happens is this: the mind is

working like an engine with the governor off it, not only
during the conscious portions of the day, but during
sleep as well; I told Maxine the other day that I write
all night, when the world thinks I'm asleep, and when I
think I am too. But really I'm writing. Twenty-four hours
a day the mind is associating so quickly, ideas are
occurring and recurring so frequently, things are
cross-fertilizing each other in such an amazing variety
of ways, that the human body cannot really bear up under
it as a normal body should be able to bear up under
the associations and the thought processes of a "normal"
mind. But there is nothing more exhilarating or exciting.
It is the thing that makes middle age worth it all, for, as
the result of long discipline, I know what I am doing,
and I know, pretty well, what to do with what my mind
gives me. Not with absolute certainty; that is of course
impossible. But with a fair degree of predictability. And
who on earth ever has that, besides artists?

Affinity between what I do in some of the poems, like
"Falling" and "May Day Sermon," and the paintings, say,
of Mark Rothko. What I wanted to do in that period was
to make great shimmering walls of words.

Only that rage is good which ends in perfection.

More observations on bronze guitar strings versus silk and
steel. As I had supposed, it *is* much easier to play on silk
and steel. It is easier on the fingers, and one can do a
great deal of subtle work up the neck, involving complex
chords, that one cannot possibly do so easily on bronze
strings. The tone, however, is not as loud as bronze. For
certain numbers, nothing on earth can equal the
authority of bronze strings and steel fingerpicks: rags,
blue grass, and such as that: Where sound volume is one
of the central ingredients of the music, bronze is far
better; silk and steel are adequate. When one really is

playing well on a piece in which the volume is a major factor, there is just nothing as good as bronze, all-metal strings. One sits there and plays, and one feels the vibrations of the sound all the way through the back of the box into one's breastbone, and one feels that one has the right sound, at least for this particular piece. What to do about this? Well, it seems to me that the more complicated practicing ought to be done on silk and steel, particularly since silk and steel strings are better for the kind of major seventh, thirteenth, and ninth work that I am trying to get into nowadays. It is just too much of a hassle to try to get this kind of chord work clean on bronze strings. They are not as good for this kind of work, anyway; they don't sound as good. When they lose their volume, they are just very troublesome strings to play on. So in following this, we ought to keep one guitar strung with silk and steel, and one with bronze, around the house. When I travel, I should have silk and steel. And that ought to solve it; as well, anyway, as it is ever going to *be* solved.

A highly wrought language like Hopkins': what has this to do, really, with the way men think and say whatever they want to say about their lives? It is all so fancy and duded-up! As *poetry* it is very effective. But no man since the world began ever *talked* like Hopkins or like John Berryman. Might there not be some kind of intensification, though, of common speech? Something that would give it a heightening that would be believable, as speech is believable? This would have to be delicately done, for the thing one must at all costs seek not to destroy is the *plausibility* of the thing being said in this way. One would have to edge up to the boundary between inventive speech and literary, or doctored-up, language—or, in the case of Berryman, lingo—and work close to it, but never cross it. This would be extremely interesting to try. How?

I am fascinated by the possibility of this slight heightening of common speech: slight, and a little strange, but not too strange. This could be magic, and better than conventional magic, for it would be believable. This is worth anything, any risk to get. It could be the making of a whole new poetic idiom, and that is important.

I must read every word of Gerard Manley Hopkins. His mind is awfully good and the ideas he throws out—as if it were the easiest thing in the world—are always fascinating and endlessly worth exploring and putting into practice.

It is very odd, how a person can approach the doing of a thing in a way not only that he had never seen or heard, but that he never could have conceived of. When I first heard Mike Russo play the guitar, it was not that what he played was so amazing, as it was amazing *how* he played. He simply treated the guitar as a percussion instrument, breaking three or four strings a concert. But the sound that this extra kind of hell-for-leather brutality —it seemed to me that he was actually *abusing* the instrument—gave the music was a revelation to me. There is no other guitarist playing who has the sound of enormous vital urgency and *swing* that Mike has. As I say, it is not only a revelation to listen to Mike play but to *see* him play.

Most poems are poor because they do not strike that *necessity*, that strange necessity. Instead, they are content with saying "something interesting."

Poetry like the poetry of Sylvia Plath one could characterize as being poetry of the hysterical intelligence.

The best abdominal exercise is fucking.

The sound of rain coming: that small, insistent sound, the sound that one knows is going to increase. That is wonderful; there is nothing more inevitable. One knows that there is some kind of purification involved, in some way.

If I ever convert *The Indian Maiden* into a play, the main thing that I wish to project is authentic sexuality and authentic tenderness. The sexuality will be a matter of creating the aura that *surrounds* sexuality: the drama, the *individual* imagery of the sexual dream—the lifelong sexual dream that is as much a part of one's self as the color of one's eyes.

Because of the experience of last week, all over again I am appalled by the thinness of my father's experience. It has been monotonous, tiresome, and valueless because he has been essentially, passive. And he has been monumentally and not creatively lazy. I cannot imagine a more awful old age than that of the lazy man, of the passive man, who wished only "to be let alone" to do his thing. The trouble with my old man is that he never had enough energy to have a thing. If he had really been good at cockfighting, it would have been a different story. But he just did it because there was nothing in particular he wished to do other than that; it was the choice over a lot of other tiresome evils, or goods; or either, or neither. It was just something to stuff into the enormous hole of Time.

There is some little passage in J. B. Priestley's novel *It's an Old Country* about London, and about the details in the London scene that the eye picks out, that is just so devastatingly and beautifully correct that I would go and knock on Priestley's door, right now, if I knew where he lived, to tell him how much moved I was, and how much the journey that Maxine and I made to England about eighteen months ago was enhanced by what he said. I doubt very much if anyone else has been touched or could be touched so much by this little thing as I have been. But the whole magic of art is there; it is in that.

I have read some bad poetry in my life. Donald Hall is bad, awfully bad, and funnily bad. Robert Bly is bad. Sylvia Plath is bad—awful, indeed. But the worst I have ever read is Tom Clark. One would have to see the stuff to believe it. And then, one would not believe it.

The trouble with most poetry, the trouble with most poems, is that they are too full of brilliant things. The poet says a brilliant thing, then he says another brilliant thing, another and another and another. There is always some sense in which these brilliant things fight each other. What the really great poet does is work toward one overwhelming image or action. He creates a wholeness, in which the elements do not clash, and so leaves the reader with one overwhelming impression rather than a series of striking fragments.

To be precise and reckless: that is the consummation devoutly to be wished.

Lowell and his followers. The young now have had too much of agony, too much self-abasement. They wish to open up, and to get at whatever wholeness there may be for them. They need a poetry which will enable them to love, which will let them love, and be affirmative and accepting of their one human life.

Line of the Australian poet Alister Kershaw:
   "Are we enough?"

I want to work more now with dialogue forms in poetry. A great deal is capable of being done here. I had the first inkling of something like this from reading Horace

Gregory's poems, long since forgotten, and probably pretty much forgotten by Gregory himself. But what he did in some of these dialogues pointed the way for me to do something *else,* I think.

Write to Karl Shapiro and tell him that I am with him in his lonely struggle.

She lies in Glendale, in Forest Lawn.

Teaching a course in poetry: a course in poetry, either writing it or reading it, becomes a course in existence, pure and simple.

The skin all over you is getting old. You can look at your foot, in an off moment, and it is not the foot you ever had before.

Will "The Indian Maiden" ever be written? I don't know. I don't know. Maybe there is too much there; maybe too much. I am terribly, terribly afraid.

There is the element of play, and fun, and improvisation, and escape. No one can tell me that this is not important. This, Robin Jarecki and I had. We were like children who had discovered sex and literature together, I at the age of forty-three, she at twenty-nine. I think of this as the true glory, at least for me. It was doomed, but not doomed in the way that it ultimately *was* doomed. I sat at my official desk at the Library of Congress, and Ruth Felt called me—a strange voice—and said, "I'm afraid I have some bad news for you. Robin died last Monday."

But we must not lose our dead.

Am I getting back into the terrible morbid nostalgia of the romantic poets, with all the emphasis on Robin now?

I don't know, and I don't care. *Es muss sein. Es muss sein.* It must be. It must be.

What matters is that Robin and I tried to make some kind of life, which was really outside of life. We tried to make something with the tools that we were allowed, and they were pitiful indeed. But we tried, and for a while we did. A very little while indeed, but that is what life tells us we must be content with. Why should this be? It must be. It must be.

My God, to hold that big sweaty body in my arms again!

She lies in Glendale, in Forest Lawn.

It is too late.

I am now close to forty-seven years old. The only question of any importance at all is how shall I spend the rest of my life. It is a whirlwind: a whirlwind. But is it the *right* whirlwind?

This notion of speeded-up and excited time: where does this lead? Alcohol helps the sense of this, but one also has a sense of time running out, and running out much faster than it need do. I must slow things down, some kind of way. What are the virtues and the beauties of *slow* time?

And yet, how glorious it is to create! For those few moments of a lifetime when the stream is running full and deep: those are the justification for everything.

It strikes me as being very odd, and symptomatic of a great many things, how much more important the word "pleasant" becomes as one gets older.

What I have done as a writer has been done by a combination of will, intelligence, and abandon. None is any good without the others.

Hard, intense work of the body—work that includes fatigues and the sense of defeat—is the most conclusive evidence of our own being that we could possibly have. Thank God for it. It must be pursued wherever it lies and in any form in which it appears; on water, on land, or in the air.

After all these years, I don't know whether the stuff I come up with should be called poetry or not. I simply call it linear writing.

Marshall McLuhan is one of these people who have no true originality, no real penetration of insight, and who try to compensate—or, in his case, overcompensate—for their lack of originality by verbiage.

Another possible title for the new book of poems: *War Embrace*.

New concept for poetical compositions: *dimensioning*.

My purpose as a poet, insofar as other people are concerned, is to liberate into the depths, not into the surfaces.

All the revolutions and the revolutionary activities of the past ten or fifteen years have been protests of the increasing trivialization of life. One thrashes around like a creature caught in a wire net to escape the enormous emphasis on trivia, on the inconsequential. This is why the journeys to the moon are important: for once, we all say, or feel, here is something, at last, that is not trivial. But what must be seen is that this enormous and impressive "step for mankind" is a *triumph* of the trivial. We all want to think large thoughts. But the question that hangs before us no matter which way we turn is this: what is *not* trivial? Well, what isn't? But we all feel—and we cannot live without feeling—that there are some things which are not. What are they?

What the American male detests most is his life of continual apology.

The ability to cut away the literary frills and affectations and to say something necessary: that is the mark of a great writer.

Poem about differences in pressures: to be called "Whose Heart Bursts."

I must let youth go, and liquor with it. To me liquor is youth, since I don't have the right, slight number of years anymore; but I must find something better.

I can't imagine anyone going through such agony and terror, but I don't know where they come from, or if they come from anywhere.

I am not what I seem to the world to be; a fine-looking fellow in the prime of life, big enough and strong enough to do almost anything he wants to do, a talented writer and the rest. No; I am a haunted artist like the others. I know what the monsters know, and shall know more, and more than any of them if I can survive myself for a little while longer.

If I could cease this fanatical introspection, I might be saved. What would I be like, then? But if I did forgo —if I could—the introspection, the putting of things into words, I should not be a writer, and that I will not give up. I cannot. The demon will not let me go and I do not believe I would go even if he would. The high moments are too good, they are too great. They are the justification for it all. I will take the rest, if I have to.

I have self-dramatized myself out of myself, into something else. What was that other thing I have left? I don't know, but this is better; it can do something.

With age, the only thing that matters is one's perversions. Let the world say what it will. Any human being who has ever lived a life on this planet knows that this is so.

There can be another kind of formalism in poetry than that which is usually and traditionally called formalism. To invent a new formalism is part of my present task. Nothing can exist without form of some kind. There are forms which are self-realized and there are forms which are trying to be formed. But the *form* of form, its invention, is another thing indeed. That is where I now want to work.

I could never be part of any movement or group.

I cannot stand myself when my belly is full of food.

Long deathwatch with my father. Nothing in his wasted and lovable life has ever become him so much as when he moved close to death. It is astonishing to understand that one's father is a brave man: very brave. The only thing he worried about was my seeing him in that condition. He cannot ever understand, whether he lives or whether he dies, how much better he looked with his arms full of tubes, with one of those plastic hospital things in his nose, and the rest of it, than at any time I have ever seen him before. He was a man up against an absolute limit, and he was giving as well as he got and he was afraid of nothing in this world or out of it. God bless that man. No matter how I came from him, I hope that it was in joy. For the end is courage.

How can one possibly hurt in so many different places at the same time?

Doctors only tell me to do that which I cannot possibly do. My only hope is to gamble on their knowing nothing whatever about what they are telling me. There is sanction for this. With me, it is called hope.

If I slowed my life down, and lived more like an ordinary person, I might live a very long time and this is supposed to be the desired object of all human life. But it is not. The main thing is to ride the flood tide. Only a few get a chance to do this and one year of it is worth a thousand years of mediocrity.

My God, I feel rotten. What is wrong with me this time? I don't know, but I can shore it up with will; I have done it so many times before.

Isn't there anything I *want* to do, anymore? No; only what I have to do.

I am Lewis; every word is true.

I don't believe I can take on another sustained work now. I don't believe it; especially as slowly as I write. But I might because it is in my head, I can see it, and must write it, slow or fast, or whatever.

The metaphor is the easiest of all devices by which to bring about a condition of falsehood. Consequently, one must be very wary of using the metaphor: it has *got* to be great, and necessary, and unexpected, and absolutely one's own.

What is coming to me in the next ten years? A decade of physical horrors. I must match them with triumphs, even though these are only triumphs to myself. Therefore it is doubly true that they must be *real* triumphs, whether they are the triumphs the world acknowledges or not.

There are so many bright people around that it is impossible to count them all. Any literary magazine, even of the third or fourth order, is full of them. But I know something they don't know, which is the reason they write about me. My business is not to question this, but to go on with what I have been doing and to do some other things too. That is the only vision of joy I have left, but it is very, very powerful.

A man cannot pay as much attention to himself as I do without living in Hell all the time.

A man like D. H. Lawrence, who will *not* have the world as it is, but wants to change everything about it, everything about the way men and women take themselves and each other, is quite simply dooming himself to perpetual frustration and rage and ultimately to destruction. Of course Lawrence would not have been Lawrence if he had been any other way, but he doomed himself just as surely as if he had taken a knife and cut his throat. There is surely a lesson in this. Change can never come as Lawrence wished it to come. Anyone who thinks otherwise is simply flying in the face of the most obvious facts of history, of society and of the impacts of individuals upon these things.

For some reason no one cares anymore about the builder of solid novels. A writer like James Gould Cozzens is pretty much cast down and out by the latter-day reviewers. Yet he is far and away the best novelist of his sort that we have. *Guard of Honor* is one of the most brilliantly constructed books in American literature.

Apparently, Cozzens is disliked more for the rather
unpleasant and illiberal personality that appears in his
books than for the novels themselves. I have just read
Morning, Noon and Night, and it has some brilliant things
in it; things which will be remembered a long time after
such ephemera as *Catch-22* are forgotten. I cannot
understand the attraction of novels like Heller's book: I
thought it was the most sophomoric and inept,
trying-for-it piece of silliness I have read in years. The
movies keep trying to do things like it, things by writers
who are something like Heller, among them Terry
Southern, and they are all dismally unfunny, at least to me.
I hope I can be warned in advance when a book or a
movie is written or made out of such persuasions as these,
so that I can do something else that evening or that week.

A phrase from Cozzens: It was too wonderful for me.

All of W. H. Auden's work, both in poetry and in
prose, has been made possible by his ability to generalize
and reason creatively.

A yellow light on a large spread of water is the most
beautiful still object I know. The most beautiful moving
object is a river. Odd that both of these should be
water-images.

All the tiresome business about diet that one reads, for
example in ladies' magazines, seems to me to be very
silly and beside the point. They are all designed to give
you the illusion that you are getting something delicious to
eat and losing weight at the same time. That is not really
possible. If you eat something that you enjoy eating you
want enough of it to satisfy you, and of course this is
too much. The Dickey Diet is very simple indeed. First
you have to be honest with yourself about wanting to lose
weight; the rest is easy. In the morning eat a little—just
enough to kill the hunger pangs—and quit eating and get

up from the table and go about your business. *What* you eat is really not important; the point is to eat just a couple of mouthfuls of something to keep from getting the hunger sickness. At noon eat a bowl of jellied consommé and drink a glass of water. In the evening eat a couple or three radishes and maybe a cracker; again, just enough to kill the hunger pangs. Then go to bed. Get up and do the same thing the next day, and the next and the next after that until you attain the weight you want. This is really not as hard as it may sound. The main thing, it works.

The best way to live in America is to be in a position to flout its values and enjoy its money.

In the projected movie, *The Small Voice*, have a scene where the poet and the girl sit down deliberately to sample each other's generation's vices: he tries marijuana, and she tries liquor. This could be terribly funny and I have no doubt it will be. They then go out to get something to eat and the girl, who has been a cheerleader in a small town, turns flips, does handstands, and so on, as the middle-aged poet woozily tries to introduce some decorum into her actions. All this in a place like Berkeley where nobody pays any attention to what she is doing except the poet.

Some kind of unknown creature lives in our lake. I saw him go by this morning, headed south, about six-thirty, and will wake Maxine in the morning so that we can watch him together. Great to see him swimming through the yellow light of dawn, on the water. One understands something unknown before.

Sound-image words, such as Brewster Ghiselin uses so skillfully, is something I want to investigate. Such words as: "Vroom" and so on. It might be fun, and instructive, and useful, to make up some of these.

Guitar playing very good, especially when I am sober. In about another ten years I will be able to do whatever I want with the instrument. At that time I will be fifty-seven years old. But so what? Gary Davis is about seventy-two and he is by far the best guitar player around, particularly of the kind of guitar player that I like best. I look forward to the bearing of the fruits of the long, devoted discipline. This is something I love very much; it is as close to me as any mode of action there is. The only thing that worries me is some kind of injury to my hands, or arthritis. But that will be as it will be. Meanwhile, I will keep on playing as though nothing were going to happen. Probably it won't, anyway.

Much is written of the "quality of life"—or lack of it— in America. Surely there is something very wrong. But I don't believe it is really necessary to have a perfect society in order to make one's own life flower. Americans for some reason, perhaps understandable, wish society to give them this mysterious quality that will make it all worthwhile. I don't believe that, and never have. The point is, to make your life as you would have it. Of course this takes money. But that, America furnishes more easily than any other society in history. With money, one can pretty much do as one pleases, though the getting of money is likely to be rather time-consuming. But with money one can give the quality of life the characteristics individually wished for. And, if one desires the society of others, there are always people with whom one is congenial. And that, as far as I'm concerned, about sums up my position on the famous quality-of-life-in-America question. Of course there is a great deal more to it than that, from society's standpoint. But not from mine.

Abstract art bores me, mostly. So does religious art. I think that a day in the Uffizi Gallery in Florence is one of the most sheerly wasteful employments of time there is. Whatever might speak to the human spirit there has surely been left out of *my* spirit.

I love colors, though; just colors.

I sympathize, in the main, with the Negro's predicament. That is, until he begins to talk about killing me and my kind. I don't think sympathy extends that far, nor should it. I will not suffer anyone to do me and my family bodily harm to right all the wrongs in the history of mankind. This would not right them, anyway; that seems obvious enough. You don't injure a person because of injuries that that person's ancestors have done you. A Negro is a black man. He insists on having "Black Pride." Why should not a white man be allowed "White Pride"? Many Negro militants would say, I suppose, because they have oppressed another race and have nothing to be proud of therefore. But this is a drastically simplistic view. Has not the white man done anything in his whole history but oppress Negroes? He *has* oppressed them and still does oppress them, but that is not the whole of his history. For better or for worse, he has built the world. Many people would say that it has been for worse, but this cannot be wholly true, for every other nation in the world wants what America has. There is enough empirical evidence to support this view in looking at one European or Oriental city for one second. Look at Tokyo, for example, striving toward Western ways with every muscle in it. No; America is *successful*. The quality of life may not be what people desire, but the standard of living ultimately determines the success and the longevity of the culture. We are pleasure-mad, but we have the best medical care in the world, and this, by very far. We have our troubles, but the main point is that finance capitalism, volume turnover, and heavy industry have brought the prosperity that we have, and that everybody else wants. There is really no other way, or at least as has yet been devised. We must live with it, and improve areas of it, but the basic *fact* of capitalism is going to last as long as there are Americans who benefit by it, or have benefited by it or hope to benefit by it.

I read a brief excerpt from a book by Tom Hayden, one of the so-called Chicago Five. The projection for the future which he and his "cohorts" and "youth" will build is absolutely and genuinely horrifying to me. Hayden speaks of "our free stores, our people's parks, our dope and our free bodies" and I, quite simply, hope that I am gone from this earth before I have to live under such conditions as that. I esteem privacy too much, and I esteem sex and true intimacy too much, to have much joy in contemplating Hayden's utopia of drugs and fornication. The trouble is that there is no dignity and decency or wholesomeness in it. I think too much of my body to offer it around just to anybody or to keep it un-lucid with drugs. Reality is drug enough for me. I detest people who try to proselytize for drugs or offer philosophical reasons as to why it is desirable to use them. That way lies a particularly ignoble form of useless madness, and any society which seriously intends to include this *part* of itself is not only stupid, but very silly as well. What are we supposed to look forward to, as the millennium? Wandering around a "people's park" in a drug trance, stepping over couples fucking wherever they wish? God deliver me and God deliver the deluded people who think this would be desirable.

Hayden also talks about "free stores." What the hell are those? Did you ever try to manufacture goods for a free store? Who would pay for getting the work done?

Or are people supposed to work for the joy, comradeship, and so on? This goes against everything that has been a part of man's mental makeup from the time of the caves. Communism, of whatever kind, simply will not work. It may work in small groups—hence the "commune"—but I doubt that it even works very well there. Suppose one of the people in the commune is a guitar player. He has a good instrument. Suppose he wants to practice at a certain time every day. But suppose another member of the commune is not a very good musician and cares nothing whatever for this other man's instrument. In a share and share alike situation he is just as much entitled to play the guitar, even to misuse it, as the man who truly loves and honors the instrument. What is wrong with the man's *owning* the instrument that he cares so much for? I don't think that this is selfish at all. Sure, capitalism probably promotes selfishness, but selfishness itself promotes a great many goods. The point is not to banish selfishness, which cannot be done anyway without banishing the human race, but to keep it from being destructive on a large-scale basis: that is, to turn it into channels that are not only materially profitable but profitable in other ways as well. This can be done; it is done all the time.

May the lord deliver me from those people whose own intelligence makes them more miserable than they need be. If intelligence and imagination are not releases into joy and fulfillment, it is better not to have them.

Ecstasy, and the continual need for it via alcohol and the insistence on living on the so-called "higher planes" of existence, killed James Agee. Ecstasy is a drug; one must learn the virtues and the creative possibilities of boredom. Likewise, Randall Jarrell was killed by his own intelligence, by overconcern for things, by frustration brought on by these matters, and by the aging process,

which intelligence made more intolerable for him than it
need have been. There are lessons here, there is no doubt.
I must learn to reject the ecstasy that I have longed for
all my life and have only recently learned how to attain,
sometimes with alcohol and sometimes without. I must go
through a slowdown period, and try to become slower
and deeper, and operate on more of a consistent human
psychological level than being very high or very low
allows me to be. I should think this would give a certain
number of advantages which I have not yet been able to
understand fully.

Use of the past participle as an adjective: "the dissolved
sea."

Just read Logan Pearsall Smith's *All Trivia*, and I reflected
how I had come into possession of the book. I got it just
after I got out of service in 1946—it was published in
1945—because of a review in *Time* which I had seen on
the boat, *Sea Devil*, on which I returned from Japan.
Books, especially poetry books and what I took to be
philosophy books, were fascinating to me then, in an
entirely different way from the way in which they are
fascinating to me now. When I got to Atlanta, even before
I was released from service, I ordered this book, and it
came in a couple of weeks. I have now taken it down
and read through it, and I must say I like it a good
deal. It is strange, is it not? How things once written
down, long ago, by people long since dead, find their
way to, say, a place like Columbia, South Carolina, across
the lake from Fort Jackson. The strange odysseys of
books, of words.

More and more I see myself as the poet of *survival*.

The trouble with most poetry, quite simply, is that it
is too much like poetry: too damn much.

Have been reading Elinor Wylie, a poet I had never really encountered before. She is very good indeed, and the proof of her value is that she has none of the raw vitalism that I esteem most in poetry—or at least, thought until now I esteemed. She doesn't have this, and I still like her. She has something else.

I have been asked to give the Phi Beta Kappa poem at Harvard during this commencement. I am working through the poems of Trumbull Stickney, and will weave together some images and lines of his and my own reaction to them and commentary upon them. This could be a very wild thing, and I must hold out for that kind of conjunctive wildness. I am fairly sure, at this early stage of things, that I am going to end with Stickney's great line about "Apollo springing naked to the light." But in my commentary this will be the Apollo rocket taking off for the moon. The end of the poem may have something to do with Stickney's brain tumor, that he "killed by dying." The end of the poem will be a line or so of my own having to do with the "flowerless moon." The end, maybe, will be something like the image of Stickney with his arrested tumor lying underground and a man who "walks weeping on the moon," both coming together in me, and making a kind of third thing.

I have been drunk, more or less, for about the last twenty-five years. Everything I remember is colored at least to some extent by alcohol. What to make of this?

For the poem about the soldier and the girl in the white Cadillac in the rain on the field problem, we might try "Fortune" as a title.

Poem about the death of Alun Lewis: this would have something to do with the plight of the man of sensibility in war, and in the modern world. One could quote a good deal from Lewis' poems and letters, and leave it up to the reader as to whether or not it would have been worthwhile for him to have gone on, conditions of war, of the individual sensibility, and of the world being what they are.

Idea for a new book. This would be called something like *Shelves*. What I would propose to do, I think, is to read across a certain number of shelves of my library, where the books are put alphabetically, taking notes on what I read, each entry having to do with something that arrested me or gave me pause to think. Sometimes I would simply quote, and sometimes I would quote and comment. Shall I do this? Yes, I think so. Whether I would publish it or not, I don't know yet.

The world, the human mind, is dying of subtlety. What it needs is force.

The quality that makes a great writer complete—and I mean *complete*—is emotional and even physical commitment to the situation about which he is writing. There are only a few human beings who can do this.

Line for the Harvard poem: "—the sun burst from a machine."

Perhaps end the poem with Stickney's line: "be softer in your triumph or we die."

Anne Sexton and Sylvia Plath might be said to belong to the School of Gabby Agony.

In any poem of John Berryman's, there is the intolerable sense of the poet *playing:* playing with the theme, playing with the words, playing with everything in connection with the poem, and playing in rather a commonplace and literary way.

It might be a good thing for me to get a little more of the Yevtushenko bounce and verve and receptivity to experience into my own work. I need a bit more of the wild man than I have at present, though I must be wild in my own way and not in his. The new metric and a good deal of energy-language would help this, and might create an entirely new kind of voice, a new tone, and a new style. Anyway, it would be a good deal of fun to try, I am quite sure.

Phi Beta Kappa poem for Harvard commencement shaping up very well. I did a good draft of the whole thing this morning, and the Stickney quotations are working out fine. I ended up with about a hundred to choose from, and am using maybe fifteen or twenty, including one at the very end of the poem. I think this is going to turn out to be quite a good venture, and I very much hope the Harvard people will like it. I have got in some of the current preoccupation with the environment, as well as a good deal about Los Angeles, nature, space exploration, and damn near everything else except Vietnam. The point is to see if I can get all these things together under one aegis, and fuse them in a single emotional personality, employing the Stickney quotes as part of the whole emotional complex. It is a very difficult job to do, but very exciting as well. I think I can bring it off, though at this early stage I am naturally not all *that* sure.

The trouble with most reading is that 95 per cent of it escapes from you the moment it is read. On the other hand, it makes reading tedious to take dozens of notes, and slows down the process so much that you get very little read. The point is, to find some way of retaining the material that the reading makes available.

Much pleased with the six Yevtushenko translations that I have done for the Doubleday anthology. I did them

quickly, and doubtless took some liberties with the texts
that I might not have had to take. But the poems, as I
have rendered them, have a good deal of that jazzy kind
of crazy colloquialism that I identify with Yevtushenko's
work, and if I can get that, and if the poems are good
poems in English, that is about all that Yevtushenko or I
or anybody could ask for.

Back reading much French, which I never seem to get
any better at, or any worse. I get about 75 or 80 per
cent of what the writer is saying, but not all the nuances.
Some of the things I gather in this hit-or-miss fashion,
though, are so exciting that I can never have enough of
them. I must do more with German and Italian. I have a
certain mediocre gift for languages.

In poetry I want a kind of deep clarity.

One of the most important things to do in poetry is to
develop a *characteristic* rhythm: a rhythm that is
characteristic of the writer, and at the same time
characteristic of the poem.

A poetry of the sympathetic vibrations between things:
for example, the sounds made by guitar strings vibrating
in sympathy with the roar of an Apollo rocket blast.

The worst kind of literary critic is the one who won't or
can't open up to the work he is reading, who refuses to
read it other than in the light of his own preconceptions.

On some of the new poems you are doing, fill the master
word list with energy-words.

The statement that I would make about almost all the
poetry I read is: "Interesting but not essential." What is
this essentiality? Each really good poet finds it in his
own way, or thinks he does.

I would characterize the work of Donald Barthelme as cute trash.

I am sick of self-effacing poetry. It is time we got some glory back into it.

In poetry, as in guitar playing or anything else, after a certain point one spends one's time trying to eliminate the little fuck-ups.

What a *weapon* poetry is! If you are immersed in it long enough, you know damn near everything. And if you like, you can use it as you wish, for whatever purpose.

If I were going to tell one of my sons how to possess the world, I would simply bring him into my house, show him that solid wall of books, and say to him: "The secret is in there somewhere, and even if you never find out what it is, you will still have come closer than if you had never read these."

When you play the guitar, emphasize that passionate, driving, excessive quality that you can hear in your music every now and then. This is a quality that one does not find very much in guitar playing, and it should be developed. When done with clean technique, it is devastating.

Timing is drama, either in music or in poetry.

Have been reading the diaries of Cesare Pavese. I find them extremely intelligent and extremely pretentious. The entries of Pavese are precisely what one detests in intellectual people. Most of what he says comes down to the necessity for "the press of body against body." This is what any truck driver wants, and has, without all the

pretentious intellectualizing about it. My God, how
tiresome literary people are, with all their scab-picking
self-importance!

I saw Robin Jarecki in a dream last night—a long, long
dream—but she was someone else and seemed not to know
me.

No one will ever be able to reconstruct my life. It is
more complicated and more unknowable than that of
Lawrence of Arabia.

I must now make a timid entrance back into philosophy,
taking notes and pondering things. Why?

Most poets have nothing to write about.

Almost all poets have very ordinary lives. They attempt
to make ordinary experience important, but almost
invariably fail. It *isn't* important, and they can't make it
so. It is that "making it so" that distinguishes the real
poet from the thousands and thousands of would-be
literary hacks that fill up the magazines. The "making it
so" is the real magic. Many are called, but few are
chosen.

All this agony, all these endless decisions about words, all
this time spent, is going to end up as nothing but books
on a shelf. It may very well be that no one will ever
touch them. They may stand there forever, upright and
dead.

I have been reading a couple of books, more or less at
random. One of these is a German book which, translated
into English, is called *Fire and Blood*, by Ernst Jünger,
and the other is a contemporary novel named *Play It As*

It Lays, by a Los Angeles writer named Joan Didion.
Jünger is a far greater writer than Joan Didion because
he is not limited to interpreting the world as it imposes
itself on the writer. Joan Didion is incarcerated in Los
Angeles, the movies, and neurosis. Jünger has a vision,
not of how things are, but of how he would have them
be. He imposes his vision on the world, and is not
dictated to by it. And that is a very great difference
indeed. It is not enough to guarantee the supremacy of a
writer, of course. But if the writer has a large vision, it
will carry the day over writers like Joan Didion, who are
brilliant whiners; they do not dominate, and Jünger does.

Poems which have imaginative power but no human power.
There are too many poems like that being written now.

Which one of us does not want to be delivered from
sex, and would not commit suicide if he were?

The great thing about not drinking—the *greatest* thing—
is that when you have a good feeling or a good idea,
you can truthfully say it is not false.

If my poetry has done anything, it has resulted in an
increase of both sensitivity and drama in American poetry.

A whole new world of poetic expression lies out
there somewhere. Or several of them, or many. These
can be experienced and explored one after the other, or
simultaneously, or they can be mixed.

New poems: "Kangaroo Hunter," "The Other Voice,"
"Polar Bear," "Mules." The last of these is about my
father's ramblings as he approaches death.

Poetry is only a man speaking to another man, if he
could.

The trouble with the poets of my time is that they have no *language*. They have simulated languages, or tongues, but no real language.

Poem: "The Home." This must be about a nursing home for the old, in which my father resides until he dies.

In the poetry of Ted Hughes most of the images are of one or two types. Something is either locked or set, and against this is played something bursting, rolling, and above all *moving* in some way. Though this is effective in a number of poems, it is a device like any other, this playing off against the set and the locked or the gripping against something which is volatile and in motion. An overreliance on this device reduces Hughes's poetry to a formula, like many another. A better poet than Hughes would use this much more sparingly, and get out into a freer universe of exchange.

I have just figured out why it is that so many people bore me. It is that they have no *style*. I don't mean affectation; I mean style. That is the difference.

Hunting season coming up again, and there is always the strange excitement. Bought Kevin a bow, some field points, and myself a bow and another kind of bow quiver. There is nothing like the excitement of the perennially unsuccessful hunter! But the idea of getting out in the fields again, a thing I do only once a year, of walking all day, of finding deer tracks, and the rest, is unbelievably exciting to me. If a biographer or someone else knew the horrible extent of my unsuccess, my so-called hunting activity would seem ludicrous, and could be made to seem pathetic, which in some ways, I guess, it is. That does not matter to me at all. I know how I feel, and what I want to do, and what I feel right doing, and consequently what I *will* do.

There are poets like Kathleen Raine who have admirable
sentiments but no subject matter at all. Miss Raine writes
about the universe, about eternal process, and so on, but
the work has no personal immediacy, no relationship to the
body, really. This is too bad, for her poems have given
me a very great deal of pleasure. But they are not really
memorable; certainly not as memorable as poems by lesser
poets which have a touch of blood and flesh in them.

Patrick Sky here for the last couple of days. He is a
"professional" guitar player and folknik. All very well and
good, and he plays some nice things. The trouble with
the Patrick Skys of this world is that they are not
professional enough. He does not really know music, has
only a middling-good feeling for it, and can pick up
new pieces only by rote. But surely the point about
being a musician is to be able to frame things and do
things your own way. This means that one *knows* the
instrument, and not just knows a little part of it. Patrick
Sky is not willing to put in a lifetime on the guitar,
really learning its intricacies and its possibilities. What he
has picked up has been picked up by means of the
so-called folk process, which is good up to a point and
beyond that point is no good. I believe in learning it
wherever you can find it, even if this includes being able
to read music and going to conservatories. If I were a
musician, that is what I would do.

Good sleep the past few nights, for which I thank all the
gods there be. The nervous crisis has left me.

Auden does not give you the feeling of experience—
experiencing—that I want my poems to give.

There is no drama like the sexual drama: the sheer
effectiveness of the human presentation and participation
is overwhelming. Looked at as a spectacle in which one

has one's *self* participating, it is the most entire delight that can be had.

Poetry seen as a *transfer* of human experience.

The device that I want to use in the new novel is one in which Cahill *will* tell the whole story, instead of shifting the point of view back and forth between several of the characters as I had previously planned to do. The story will be told in the third person, but everything will be "seen" from Cahill's perspective. The point will be that Cahill interprets the world in mental images, based upon what he has seen previously: that is, all the images in his mind that he remembers, has read about, has dreamed, and so on, when he was able to see. Everything he "sees" at the primary flying school where his son was killed will be "seen" by means of these previously perceived mental images. This will be awfully difficult to do, but, if successful, will be very striking, and maybe something new in the novel form.

The whole concept of understanding exactly what placement a word has in a poem is becoming more and more important; the trouble is that most people do not have acute enough sensibilities to understand what has been done. For example, the translation of a poem by García Lorca opens with the lines "The New York dawn has . . ." What is it that the New York dawn *has?* The whole use of this simple verb opens up a universe of correspondences and verbal imagery and discourse that nothing else would do in quite the same way. Such a principle must be thoroughly understood, and almost never is.

What the best kind of imaginative woman loves most about a man is his depraved and marvelous side. The same could be said about what men love about women:

the air of complicity; what Jünger typifies when he says that there is the attitude of "Now, no nonsense! This is just between us beasts."

It is thought by Americans that having enough money—or a lot of money—guarantees a good life no matter what the locality, the tradition, lack of it, or whatever. But that is not so. People with money, but with no tradition behind them, do not live as *well* as people with money and with a definite tradition of behavior, of cookery, and of the other things that tradition makes possible. I have seen a lot of rich people of both kinds, and this is a very definite conclusion. It is tradition that makes money *work* well: that is, work for the enhancement of life rather than simple pleasure, dissipation, and so on.

The excitement about another *person* is the greatest human excitement of all: better than excitement about landscape, about politics, about God, or about anything else.

There is a fundamental difference between what I am trying to do in poetry and what Pound and Eliot were trying to do. They were trying to interpret culture in one way or the other. I am not trying to interpret; I am trying to *give* to people. This may sound rather too much as though I were trying to give myself the best of the comparison. That may be so; nevertheless, it is true.

I hereby declare an end to self-terrorism. The remedy for this condition that has plagued me so long is work, and plenty of it, some physical and a great deal of it mental.

A poem does one of two things. Either it stands still and describes or elaborates, or it moves. It moves *from*

something *through* something *to* something. It starts
somewhere and it comes out somewhere.

The true feeling of sex is that of a deep intimacy, but
above all of a deep complicity.

The kind of poetry I like most is extreme, simple,
passionate, and imaginative.

Poetry magazines and anthologies and bookstores are filled
with the work of fairly talented, fairly interesting
period-style workmen. That is why a really distinctive
poet stands out so strongly; it is the contrast. Not one
poem out of a hundred thousand that are being presented
weekly and monthly and yearly will survive. It is hard to
tell what the qualities that enable such a poem to
survive are, but it has something to do with the stamp of
a unique personality upon it. This is indispensable, and it
is why all the secondary poets, the little Robert Lowells,
the little Audens, can do nothing but make the Lowells
and the Audens loom larger, for these others perform the
service—perhaps dubious—of pushing them up higher
with their accumulated efforts. Maybe this is as it should
be, maybe not. But this is the way it seems to be. As
for me, I am sick of my imitators, but I cannot repudiate
them; after all, I made them possible, for better or worse.

There is first the insight—large or small—and then the
way of phrasing it.

Mark Van Doren is vastly underrated as a critic, and
even more underrated as a man. He is one of the truly
luminous presences among us. Surely men will know this
after he is gone; a few know it before he leaves.

The meditative poet and the poet of action. This does
not mean, necessarily, that an action is *depicted* in the

poem, but that the words themselves contribute to a
sense of action ultimately physical. They are those *kinds*
of words.

Nowadays, apparently, everyone has to have a kind of
archetypal saint from earlier movies. James Wright's,
for example, is W. C. Fields, which is fairly standard.
Mine is Wallace Beery, who combines sentimentality and
savagery, and above all, a quality of incomprehension.
All this is lovable, hateable, and very hard to understand,
as existence itself is. But Wallace Beery is a formidable
figure in a way that W. C. Fields is not. He is much more
humanly believable.

One can get very tired of the frantic in poetry. I have
just bought a number of books in England, and am now
reading them. Ted Hughes is frantic; Peter Redgrove is
frantic. It won't do.

The direction indicated by the "Pine" poems is the one I
want to explore now. This kind of associational imagery
of a very special and wide-ranging sort can be applied to
subjects either small or large, short or long. The
thing may have tremendous depth and suggestibility. But
I don't understand it yet.

The problem now is to make an extremely imaginative,
sometimes farfetched metaphorical idiom humanly
convincing at the same time. If I can solve this, an
entirely new kind of poetry will be born.

The phrase "fountain light."

The first prerequisite for a great poem is a great *concept*
for a poem.

It seems to me that there has been no poetry written yet,
at all.

Yesterday a woman graduate student came up to me after class and said, "You are the most wonderful man I have ever met." That may be true, but what I said in return was even more true, and equally sad. I said, "No; but you have married yourself to a man who cut off your possibilities."

What we all want is savage delight.

There is so *much* unrhymed verse around. What does this mean? Only that a good many of the less talented people are lazy, and just like to write in chopped-up prose. But I myself am writing mostly unrhymed stuff now. What does this mean? It means that the *rhythm* must be worked harder than the prose-verse people work theirs.

Mark Strand's poetry strikes me as essentially silly, being a simple-minded kind of exercise in deliberate eccentricity. A lot of verse nowadays is like his. The trouble with it is that it is not grounded firmly or deeply enough in ordinary reality. All good poems start and end there, and go through something else in between.

Something either sickening or marvelous happens when one human being puts his hands on another in any way at all.

An entirely new poetry. The poetry of murderous drives.

For example, pertaining to the last entry: the business of being terrified of what one will do: that is, maybe, throw a girl off a cliff. But when one comes to stand with the girl at the edge of the cliff, all one really feels is a vast desire to *protect*.

Work is easy. The thing that makes it hard is persuading yourself that it is hard.

I am coming into that place where literally everything
is poetry. There is the place to be.

I want, maybe, to write poems of raw imagination and
not of form.

A great deal of poetry has nothing whatever to do with
reality: that is, *anybody's* reality. It is a verbal construct
merely. The good or great poetry, though, has
something to do with reality. Poets should never forget
that reality—what *is*—is the great mother of all invention.
The poem should come of reality and go back into it.
But it should *impose* itself on fact.

The blazing clearness. The blazing clearness. How to get
it?

Most poetry is what one might call poetic bullshit. How
to avoid this? But on the rare occasions when one does
avoid it, and can avoid it, real poetry is possible, just
barely.

One of the most tiresome of all literary affectations is
that of the willfully original. British writing is full of
this.

Lowell is the kind of American poet that the British will
"settle for" as being significant. That is, they can
understand him, and they can handle him, in the bitchy
gentlemanly reviews that they write. They cannot stand
being shook. There are many ways in which they can get
around being shook, and the foremost of these is to take
in an American poet like Lowell, or, better still, Sylvia
Plath. This is all very tiresome, but it happens. They
settle for entirely too little. And they attempt to exalt a
journeyman British poet like Ted Hughes. That won't
wash. Poetry is far more magnificent and far beyond

anything that would encompass these mediocre people as ends. The beginning has not even been sighted yet.

The excitement of the mind. Yes, the *excitement* of the mind!

If it should happen, and it does happen, that I become apologetic about the range of my interests and the peculiar nature of them, all I need to do is to think about T. H. White, who was so much greater than I am in this regard, so much *more* interested, so much more learned, so much more loving of so many different things.

A wonderful short dream this afternoon of sand, ocean, and some kind of duplicity involving myself and two girls. I have very rarely had a nicer time. What dream tonight?

Liberty and frankness.

Or rather, liberty, frankness, and significant imagination. That's it.

The real creative writer is caught between the tongs of a nutcracker. First, he must realize that the words that he puts down on a piece of paper will stay the way he has put them. But it is also true that if he allows *those* words to stand, no *other* words can be in that particular place in his composition, or take up that identical space. This is very inhibiting, at least to me. It is especially so when one realizes that the full, fine leap and flight of the spontaneous imagination is the one thing he must rely upon, particularly at the beginning of whatever he is trying to write. So . . . how to get these two things together: the inhibiting presence of the idea that one is *stuck* with whatever words one decides to leave in their places, and the reliance on spontaneous invention? But there are ways of getting these two elements to work in conjunction, at least occasionally.

Be more systematic—a lot more systematic—about what you do with incoming material: the new stuff. I have lost literally hundreds of good poems through stashing them around in places where I never look, and consequently forget what I have done with them.

Work out the new idiom of "country surrealism."

There are many *idiomatic* discoveries that can be made. And I think that possibly this is the key to a real originality of style, something never done before. There can be many of these, and it should be great fun and very exciting to explore them.

Missed hunting this year, and it made me very sad. I had all the equipment, new arrows, new bow, and so on, but I didn't have the time. Maybe I could take Kevin and go up to Alaska or western Canada on some safari-type trip later on, next year. Write to people about the possibility of this.

It is very disturbing indeed when you can't think of any new perversions that you would like to practice.

Lean hard on the technique that you have come to call "country surrealism," and develop it for whatever it can be made to do. In connection with this, write some poems about *invocations:* poems in which one thing *calls* to another, commands it, makes demands of it, and so on. Could be, if done right, absolutely hair-raising.

The word lists I make are a way of getting new words into the poem. I tend to use the same ones over and over again, and I am always looking for words that I am unused to using. I need those.

Berryman has to go the long way round, for that is the only way he can get to it. But a really great poet goes *straight* to it.

The most important thing you can ever possibly do as a writer is to commit yourself entirely to the imaginative conception that you have made. Whether it is a disaster, a triumph, or a commonplace, the name of the game is to get into it utterly. Everything is in that.

What I want most to do in the poem is to go for the glory, and to keep the pretentiousness out.

The thing that beats you—and that you must beat—is self-hatred.

The trouble with most poetry is that it is either too real or too fantastic. Either it is too real, verging toward the prosaic, or it is too fantastic, verging toward the impossible. It would be a very easy thing to say that the solution to the problem would be to merge these two things. But it is not. It is to do *another* thing, entirely.

There are two kinds of functional metaphors. One of them is the "that's the way it is" kind. The other is the "can it possibly be that that's the way it is?" kind.

What I want most for the poem to be for the reader is a kind of *adventure*. He should start out on it, continue, and then, end. But the sense of adventure, certainly with a good deal of *peril* entailed in it, is paramount.

I am sick of the petty wildness and the phony ecstasy of drinking. It is a relief to go back to being what I am, what I was intended to be.

I expect that the best definition of the traditional
Hollywood sex goddess is that she is a girl or a woman
who would fuck—well, even you.

There is a good deal of difference between the fanciful
and the truly imaginative. All of Robert Bly and a good
deal of Jim Wright is fanciful; fanciful only.

I am uncommonly terrified when our basketball team
loses. I find myself unable to explain this. I could see it
would be normal to be depressed, but not frightened.
Strange.

That is the trouble with most poets: they settle for a
cleverness.

In the novel, or at least in the novel as I want to write
it, the main thing has to be the *thrust:* that is, the
narrative movement. Other novelists will try to work up
a trivial incident, and overlay it with detail. That is not
what I want to do. I don't wish to take the trouble of
writing a novel unless I have clearly in my head the idea
for the novel. What I wish is a conception that I believe
will hold all the elaboration, or lack of it, that I wish to
present. I don't want to spend years in a vain attempt to
elaborate an essentially uninteresting novelistic idea.

Pursuant to the last entry: I don't want to waste time on
something that I don't believe is a winner from the
beginning. *Whole* conception before I attempt any detail
work. That is the way it was with *Deliverance*, and that
is the way it will be in any future novels of mine.

You know, it's very God damn strange. I don't believe I
could do *anything* I would approve of.

Will it ever be given to me to attain that large, free,
effortless, and essentially *simple* thing that I have wanted

all my life? But at times I have sensed it, and have been close. I wonder if this will ever be true again. Perhaps in death itself. Perhaps not.

The wholehearted *delight* in a thing! The whole question and answer, and the uselessness of both, are resolved in that. Questions and answers are, when one is in that state, irrelevant.

There are a couple of options open to the poet. The most important of these is to find a way of plunging the reader into an incident, or an occurrence, or a state of mind that *must* matter to him. The other way is much less important. That is to work up something essentially trivial *as though* it were important.

The surest sign of the aging process is that one continually looks for blood coming out of some bodily orifice.

I hope that I am through with the facile overemotionalism that I have been using for the last few years as a substitute for youth. There are far better things, deeper feelings.

If I have made any contribution to literary criticism, it is that I have reintroduced sensibility and emotion back into it.

One gets so *tired* of the truth. One wants to make another kind.

At the age of forty-eight, one becomes aware of a singular, distressing, strange, and exhilarating thing: the world and experience gets going faster and faster. Life is speeded up, the lid comes off, and one has no recourse but to go with bodily desire, imaginative abandon, delight, frustration, and death.

If you are secure in yourself you can do anything and nothing matters to you but how you feel about yourself. The Nobel Prize can go to somebody else when you think you should have got it and you can lean your right arm against an arbor and smile, knowing that whoever it was who got the Nobel Prize is not nearly so valuable to himself as you are, leaning there in the late afternoon sun.

In *Death's Baby Machine* Joel's instructor becomes obsessed with trying to give Cahill all the sensations that Joel had as a beginning pilot. Partly he does this because he's the way he is, is not subject to the draft and can leave instructing any time he wants to, and partly because of his hatred for Riker and the military. These things, and his love for flying, particularly in very maneuverable, acrobatic-type aircraft like the Stearman.

Rigorously guided relaxation—or rigorously guided abandon —is the secret to everything, from guitar playing to love-making, to poetry, to the novel—to just about everything there is, including athletics.

Something important for the new poetry: images from electricity: the *charged* flowers.

One feels so damn sorry for writers, the poor posers. People like Hemingway and Yeats spend their whole lives trying to make good a pose because they despise themselves. They put infinite time and energy into trying to make themselves come true, when they know that it's all a damn lie, anyway.

It is not what men *do* that is frightening, but what they and the human race are *capable* of. This is frightening because they don't know where it will end or if it will end, or if they will ever be able to stop themselves from the ongoing that the "scientific spirit" has impelled them into. Curiosity may well be the thing that kills the human race, because it breeds monsters.

Mademoiselle magazine has asked me to write something —three hundred words—on "Feminine Sexuality," and I guess I will try to do it. But what on earth do I know about *that* subject? Woman as flesh? meat? vision? Claudel said somewhere that woman is the promise that cannot be kept, but maybe she is kept too much. Or that may be what Claudel meant in the first place; I don't know. Anyway, I see her as something which is essentially *ideal*, and I will write my three hundred words around that notion, for it has always seemed a true one to me.

I have just received the collected poems of Robert Fitzgerald, and have read through the book with fascination and delight. I have always liked his work a great deal, though for my taste he is a little distant and cool, elegiac and learned. But Fitzgerald has a genuine insight into those scenes and people in which the "tears of things" reside. And he surely writes beautifully, coolly, and distantly about them. Very few things of his are literally unforgettable, but they are all memorable. I renewed my acquaintance with many of the poems with honor and delight. He is a good poet, very minor, but it is also likely to be true that good minor poets write better than good major poets. I think these classifications of major and minor are really kind of silly anyway. The thing that matters is not major poets and minor poets but *good* poets. Robert Fitzgerald is one of those, thank God.

Someone should write an essay called *The Sorrows of Intelligence*.

Just read Ted Hughes's book, *Crow*. That's the kind of stuff I throw away. It has nothing to do with the world. I am sure that if some British reviewer ever sees this, he will say, "Dickey would have been well advised to keep a little of it." Nevertheless, that's the kind of stuff I throw away.

What I want most in poetry is a haunted clarity.

Poets say nowadays there is nothing for us to break through to. After all, they say, we haven't a kind of straw dummy like the Georgian poets in Eliot's time to come up with something radically different than. This seems nonsense to me. Poetry, and the poetic line, are so hoked up with special effects, with people trying to be "intense" and "interesting," that the whole of poetry, almost, is entering into a period of the utmost artificiality. No wonder people don't read it; I can hardly read any of the new stuff myself. What we need, as *our* breakthrough, is a poetry of extreme simplicity, where one thing is said per line; but that thing must have almost infinite reverberations. I am not talking about a gnomic sort of utterance, but some new, modern thing. The sources of language for this sort of poetry have hardly been tapped at all. But if we can get this, poetry will have a great deal more resonance for people who never read much poetry because of the excesses of Berryman or the erudition of Empson. We need to go a different way from that now. I suspect that narrative may also have something to do with it, and if one could combine this extreme simplicity of utterance with a great deal of penetration and a narrative element of either an ultra-real or a surreal kind, he would have what is going to be the wave of the future. Either he would have it, or he would make it.

The greatest poets are those who have been able to command the greatest range of effects. Where Lowell is limited to a heavy, driving sort of paranoiac verse, and others are reduced to a trick or two of violence or oversubtlety, Shakespeare was able to go from drive to air, from banter to tragic utterance: he commanded every effect and every possibility. Surely this is the stuff of great poetry, and this is the goal to be striven for, no matter how far we may fall short of it. A *full* range, not sacrificing one thing to another, but taking them all in, in different poems.

Poem, "The Frail Craft." The one letter to the girl who has since been married, with instructions how to fold it into a paper aircraft and waft it gently out the window, toward the river Charles.

Poem: "War Books." These are the books that one takes to a war, as in the famous case of books taken to a desert island. They are a combination of what one finds at hand and what one goes desperately out to seek, through the streets of San Francisco, a day or two before sailing. This could culminate in the grand hurricane, the destruction of the library on Okinawa, and the salvaging of books which one could not have come by in any other way.

The poetry of W. S. Merwin is all the same. It lacks drama. It might be called "a poetry of interchangeable parts." He is very prolific, and this factor makes his poems seem even more undistinguishable from each other than they might be if there were fewer of them.

There are almost no poets who have any sense of the dynamics to be afforded by a real understanding of metrics, and what might be gained by metrical experimentation. Hopkins is almost the last poet to grasp this fact, and to explore it in his own way.

I have three modes of poetry that I am working in now. One is the narrative-dramatic mode that most of my work heretofore has been in. Second is the so-called "new metric." The third, the one I have done least writing in and least experimentation in, is what I call "country surrealism." Now if I can find a way to get the three of them together, I will have a wild sound, sure enough! The point is, though, to write different things in different modes, and to bring them together, at times, *very* cautiously. But there should be ways in which these three modes might be able to cross-fertilize each other. A fourth possibility is translation work and *mis*readings, from, say the German.

Another mode is the mode in which I wrote the "Pine" poems. That would give me five.

Must go down to New Orleans and be on Bill Buckley's show next week. What in the hell are we going to talk about for an hour? Anything. Everything. Nothing.

Have been reading some essays by E. B. White. He is good, but too stylized and a little mechanical, within what has defined itself over these thirty years as the *New Yorker* style. He is a bit too fey for me, though enjoyable. He is enjoyable but forgettable; regrettably, for he is someone I wanted very much to like.

Starting back to writing poetry is the most exciting thing that has happened to me recently. I have got the thing going in three or four different directions, am mixing up these directions, and experimenting all over the place. I have never had such a damn good time in my life. This is what I ought to have been doing for the past couple of years, except that the other commitments have taken me away from it. But I can see a way to do *something* in poetry every day, and that I plan to do.

A glorious spring here. Must take a lot more photographs, and in color. I have never seen such a glorious array of flowers! I have lived in Columbia for three years, but have never really *seen* it.

In *Death's Baby Machine* one of the big scenes—if not the biggest—is during the parade and air show when Zack has been killed (figure out how this may convincingly and dramatically be done) and Cahill finds himself on the other side of the field. We will previously have established that he is an advanced diabetic, which has cost him his eyesight, and he will have overinjected himself with insulin at some earlier time, and is now on the far side of the airfield with insulin shock coming over him. He must get back to the mess hall, or somewhere where he can get sugar. Meanwhile, Riker has had the instructors and selected cadets, as well as himself, start all the engines of the aircraft sitting on the flight line, and Cahill must somehow, without the aid of his dog, make his way back back to the cadet area through the whirling blades. Some of the pupils in the aircraft see him and shut their engines down, some see him but don't shut their engines down, and some are just oblivious to the fact that a blind man is trying to cross the flight line through all those whirling blades.

The first action scene of the novel will be a scene where Zack is attacked by other dogs. Another is where Cahill is literally "flying blind." The third will be, maybe, Cahill and Zack caught in a brush fire similar to the one into which Joel crashed. The fourth might be a fight between Cahill and Groome, though I have not as yet decided whether to include this. The fifth will be the scene where Cahill tries to cross back through the field of whirling propellers.

Bit of dialogue for the last page or two: The girl says something like, "Well, we're both pretty sick people." And Cahill says, "Maybe something can be done about you, at any rate." Then the girl says, "I somehow or other doubt it." And Cahill says. "Well, anyway we'll see."

Get from Gary Adelman an *exact* medical description of how he went blind from diabetes, and the exact feel of his blindness, with "a continual flashing of lights in the eyes," and that sensation of always being blinded by *light*, continuously.

One of the reasons Cahill wears dark glasses is that his eyes are continually jerking and rolling and flickering from one side to the other. Judging from Gary Adelman's eyes, this is part of that particular kind of blindness. You can tell that the person is blind when you see his eyes move so continuously and abruptly. Though Cahill has dark glasses on, he is aware of that continuous movement of his eyeballs, because he can feel it physically, and see the continuous dull flashing of light where he should be seeing images, things, the world.

At crucial places in the novel we should refer to the movement of Cahill's eyes, how he feels it at various times and show how it becomes more agitated and desperate as *he* is disturbed.

Bit of dialogue for the novel: the girl or somebody asks Cahill, "How are you going to get home without Zack?" and Cahill answers, "Oh, I think I can make it all right. I'll depend on people, I reckon."

At the end, Riker orders Cahill off the field, which, as he says, "I shoulda done a lot sooner."

Joel's instructor is named McCaig.

There is a scene where Cahill feels the strut-wires of one of the airplanes: the sensation that this gives him.

Especially in the cold, when he takes off his glove in
order to feel the wire.

There might also be a kind of seriocomic shot where
Harbelis talks Cahill through a basketball shot—Cahill was
once an athlete—and Cahill, in his hat and glasses
and overcoat and muffler, keeps trying until he sinks
one. He can tell when it goes in by the sound he
remembers, and Harbelis is jubilant.

Harbelis is Greek Orthodox. Find out something about
this church.

Harbelis has done his running and basketball playing
for church leagues.

The capacity to think up themes for stories, ideas,
conceptions, and so on depends very much on the
cultivation of doing so. The more one sets his mind
thinking, deliberately, along these lines, the more alert
one becomes to possibilities of this sort. I have been at
this so long that I honestly believe I could think up seven
or eight ideas for poems within a minute or two. This
is a fortunate situation for a writer, and I am very well
aware that it is.

Had drinks last night in Charleston with two old
homosexuals. It was a very funny conversation—they were
both antique dealers—and also very sad. But, despite their
affectations, I couldn't help liking both of them a good
deal, and enjoyed their telling me about their "good
time" in going around looking at old houses down here,
going into antique shops together, pricing things, and so
on. There was something very sweet, harmless, and
extremely innocent about the whole thing. They have a
better life than a great many people do.

I don't know yet how Zack is going to be killed, but I think it should be in a scene where there is a very great deal of confusion, and there is no precedent in the dog's life or training to enable him to know what to do. In other words, it is an accident of some sort, in which there may be some degree of maliciousness on someone's part, but the main thing is that it is a confused kind of action. It would be too obvious to suggest that Zack died from trying to protect Cahill from something, but it may be a situation in which the dog thinks something of this sort is going on, when it isn't. Anyway, work it out on that basis in the beginning, and see where that takes us.

I don't know whether or not Thomas Wolfe was a great writer—though I personally think that he is—but he is a great *something*.

Stange dream last night about a doctor who had evidently just become a friend of my mother, in some way which had to do with his riding a bicycle by her house—which is not where she lives now—every day. He was a young, athletic fellow, very hairy-chested and almost bald, and had had his left arm amputated in an accident, and in some way had had it transplanted about halfway down his side, where he had this withered little arm. He was a surgeon, and I asked him if he could use the hand on that arm, and in reply he grasped my hand weakly and tried to squeeze down on it as hard as he could, but I could just barely feel the pressure. We sat and drank Coca-Cola and talked, and he advised me to get an operation for my appendix, preferably to be done by him, but I refused, and he seemed to understand.

Wonderful trip to Charleston this weekend with family. The weather was lovely, the city was lovely, the houses and walled gardens were lovely. Everything was as lovely

as it is possible for things to be in Charleston, and that
is lovely indeed. Never before have I felt so strongly the
truth of what the character in the Harold Pinter play says,
on coming through a door on stage. He looks up, down,
and around, and then says, with wondering, hopeful
enthusiasm: "Jesus! A guy's got a chance in a room like
this!" A guy's got a chance in Charleston.

A second-rate writer like Norman Mailer will sit around
wondering what on earth it is that Hemingway had that
Mailer might possibly be able to get. A really good
writer, a genius or something comparable, does not say
anything like that at all. If he thinks about the matter, he
is likely to wonder what it is that is going to make him
unique, not what he can borrow from what some other
writer has done, either in style or in life-style. He is
going to be concerned first and foremost with what he
can *create*. If he can do this, then others will be
following him, as Mailer follows Hemingway.

I am beginning to look old, and I feel, faintly, the cold
breath of the void, for such a look is one of the bodily
things that nothing can be done about. But I feel great,
and I am down under 215 pounds. It has always been
easy for me to lose weight and I think I will go down
now to 185 just to see what happens. I will really be a
rail at that weight. Still, my tennis game may pick up,
and I could surely do a great deal more physically than
I can at 215. This should take until about the middle of
the summer, with a lot of tennis and running.

E. E. Cummings' objection to the poetry of Robert Frost
is that there is not enough *intensity* in it. I tend to agree
with this, though I like a good deal of Frost. What I
don't like in Frost is a sort of personally agreed-upon
complacency. This quality seems to have been the one

most esteemed by the American people, but I have always encountered it with the sensation of chewing on sand.

Stanley Edgar Hyman is one of the most thorough, hard-working critics to come along in my time. When he writes about something, he has researched it thoroughly, and he has definite opinions on it. He is a very entertaining critic, though, like all critics, with a number of blind spots and limitations. But I can always read him with enjoyment, whether or not I agree with him. He is stimulating, feisty, and very learned. These are good qualities, and his critical books are good, informative books, his reviews are very definite and provocative, and his scholarly works, such as *The Tangled Bank*, are, as they used to say in the back pages of the literary quarterlies, models of their kind.

Very good guitar these last few days. Quite a heartening experience. In another five years I can do what I want with the instrument, and that is something to look forward to when you are middle-aged.

Why fight this battle of time? A battle that is already lost? Well, there are ways to do it, and to make time, as they used to say in north Georgia, live hard.

Film version of *Deliverance* proceeding very well. John Boorman says he has the cast of unknowns and amateurs he wants, and I am very eager to meet them.

I need now to go into a prolonged period of experimentation: metrical, imagistic: experimentation in diction, in possibilities of word usage, and so on. It is fatally easy to fall into one's own successful style. The point is that I can write poems in the style that I have written in already for as long as the world and I shall last. There is nothing to that anymore, but it may yield

some good poems; better than the ones I have heretofore
written in that style. But the field now needs to be
broadened, and I must seek ways of doing that. I need
another kind of *sound* than that which has come to be
associated with my work; in fact, I need several of them;
as many as I can come up with, by whatever means.

Alert and relaxed: that is the secret.

The world thinks that I am a very industrious literary
man, turning out lots of work in a very short period of
time. This may be so, but the reason for it is not as
they suspect. I don't sit many hours at the typewriter,
except very rarely, when I see the prospect of
finishing something that I have been working on for a
long time. I simply do *something* every day, even if it is
just changing a punctuation mark, or a thing equally
trivial and equally vital. The point is that I am always
moving on something, and it is astonishing how much
poetry, criticism, fiction, and so on gets written under
those conditions.

In the screenplay, make sure that I get back in the part
where Ed picks up the mountaineer's gun, almost *becomes*
the man he has murdered, and sights down on Bobby
with it. I don't see how this could fail to be a powerful
and shocking scene, for everything that Ed has done has
been done alone, and a man alone will do things he
would not do if there were other people around. That
feeling is one of the most important feelings in the film,
and this scene would emphasize it as nothing else could.

It is exactly as I told Sam Peckinpah about the task of
the artist: we live to give them images: Gatsby and Daisy
with his shirts, Queequeg with his harpoon, Jake Barnes
with his woman.

A great night image that keeps recurring to me, of myself as a young uncertain guy and some girl going down long rain-wet steps with a bank of very green trees shedding green light on us as we go down.

Poem about the long hill for roller skating, and/or the driveway out of which one would come shooting as off a ski jump. This might be good, considering the fact that the automobile comprises the chief danger to the roller skater. One might also have a funeral scene of one of these skaters attended by all his small classmates; other skaters who have gone the same route and come through it alive, at the age of ten.

Poem about military men who are assigned to county fairs and other places of public entertainment to demonstrate weapons of war, to conduct little children on "parachute jumps," and such like. What must such an assignment be like? How can senior officers in all conscience give fighting men such assignments? And how do the fighting men respond to this mock warfare with children in a great place of public entertainment, at a certain place, and at a certain time, and under those carnival lights?

For the Wesleyan speech, the main motif is going to be the inexplicable "what have *I* done?" The point is that by means of this collective guilt-thing, we are all being robbed of our essential humanity, and of our lives as human beings on this earth. Of *course* steps should be taken to rectify all of these so manifest evils. What I am inveighing against is the continual put-down of the individual's response to his own life, to creation, fulfillment, and joy. It is no good to say that none of these things is ever going to come about while all of these evils are abroad. I say that if all evils were put to rest there would still be no guarantee that conditions of fulfillment would obtain within the individual life. If we wait until all wrongs are righted before we begin to live our lives fully, creatively, and joyously, then we will never *have* our lives.

Two poetic modes: the narrative and/or anecdotal, and the intensive, the timeless.

The intensive method can be brought to bear on anything on earth, as can poetry generally. It can come out of a deer-track, a rusty bridge across the Chattooga River, a highway or a supermarket or the shape of a woman's eye. The universe of time does not exist that is long enough to furnish the requisite period to cover the multiplicity of possibilities.

Thomas Wolfe is so rhetorical that it is almost a shameful act. But there should be such rhetorical writing, as the indication of a kind of limit.

I am sorry that the English critics do not think better of me than they do. American poetry is a very great deal better than English poetry at this time, and I dare say will remain so. But the English critics *cannot* admit me to the stature that I have in my own country, for that would be to betray something in themselves, and in their own writers. They don't mind acknowledging Lowell, who after all spends a good deal of time over there, and is a safe enough bet, but they will not admit an American, and more particularly a Southern, writer who challenges them. That is too bad, because I love that country, and have a good many friends there, and admire several of their writers, though these are not the ones that, with their peculiar kind of academic puffery, *they* admire. I expect that the only way I will ever get any satisfaction out of this love of England is just to go there as a tourist, and not as an American writer. This is too bad, but it has its advantages too.

I will not curry favor with reviewers, or with anybody else. They have to come to me. I surely won't go to them under any circumstances whatever.

New thresholds! New anatomies!

Nothing is hard, or no hardship comes as particularly much of a hardship, to the man who is man enough.

If we can explore and fully understand the new language and the new metric, and combine it with narrative—either real or surreal—we will have something pretty amazing, I think. But that's all to do yet.

Explore the possibility of having Cahill meet, under some circumstances or other, a blind street singer with a guitar or a record player looped around his neck. We might get a Baptist hymn or two into the novel!

Write to Chris in a letter the very obvious truth, which he surely recognizes, that he was "born for controversy." Point out to him that everything that has ever been accomplished in the arena of political and social action has come from people like himself, who were born for controversy.

I would like to hit the English reviewers with the term "self-conscious primitivism" for Ted Hughes. That is just exactly right. There is something pathetic about it; as though this were the end of all, the last-ditch stand.

Reread William Gibson's *Seesaw Log*. Many fascinating parallels between the making of the play, *Two for the Seesaw*, and the filming of *Deliverance*. I think Gibson was extraordinarily lucky in having such honest people working with him, though the frustration of having to see his play corrupted into success is agonizing.

Today found the word "find." This word could be used
so constructively and originally in a poem—as well as
the *concept* of finding and of things found—that it is
actually frightening to me. I remember something I read
of William Blake's that put me onto this train of
thinking. Blake said in his journal: "Yesterday found the
word 'golden.'"

I have always loved the writings of James Agee, because
they are so earnest and so unfailingly responsible to the
human condition. But I have been rereading his work
lately, and it seems to me, now, after many years, that
there is something overurgent about it: it is work,
whether in film, essay, prose fiction, or whatever, that
insists on your taking it seriously, beyond the other
writings that you might read. He is a fine writer, but
this quality of *insistence* on the importance of what is
being said is, ultimately, very tiring. Walker Percy is at
the opposite extreme. He is relaxed and very original—in
his way more quietly original than Agee is—but his work
does not have this desperate urgency of Agee's. Agee is
a person who can and has become the central figure of a
cult of earnest, literary-minded people. Walker Percy,
self-effacing and quiet and devastatingly original, could
never be the object of *anybody's* cult. I expect that Agee
will last longer, but I sincerely believe that Walker
Percy is the better writer.

There are writers like James Agee and Thomas Wolfe
who are more valuable as human beings than they are as
writers, and this is too bad because they are both
fiercely individual and, at times, very good writers. But
the value of Thomas Wolfe is as an example of a certain
kind of excessively reactive human being, and the value
of James Agee is something similar to that, though his
linguistic sense is much finer than Wolfe's. Wolfe's
personality, as it comes through the bumbling of his

writing, is a very valuable thing for the human race to have, both as example and cautionary example. James Agee's self-destructiveness is also important, and his marvelous attitude of *caring* so desperately much for so many things. To care as much as Thomas Wolfe did and James Agee did is to be seen as a form of self-destructiveness. They both drank heavily because they cared so much and responded so much, and drink helped them to dare and respond. Surely one can understand this. They are both great personalities, Wolfe greater than Agee, though not such a fine writer. Paradoxically, as a writer he will be remembered longer than Agee, whether or not this is good, or bad, or indifferent. Thomas Wolfe is an enormous *force*. Agee is a smaller man, a better writer, and with his own special poignancy. But he does not have the stature that Thomas Wolfe had, largely because Thomas Wolfe was able to *impose* himself on the reader in ways that Agee was not able to do. It is good that we have them both.

I must admit now that the so-called "art" film has usually bored me very much. I have never seen anything by Ingmar Bergman that I could even sit through. The pretentiousness of movies like *Virgin Spring* is such that I simply cannot stay awake. Doubtless I show myself an unresponsive moviegoer by such an admission, but it is to be admitted, even so. I feel the same way about ballet, and most particularly about modern dance, which seems to me to be the most suffocatingly pretentious kind of activity that a human being could engage in. I read Edwin Denby's work on dance, and I was almost persuaded. But finally, not.

The most successful scene that I can remember in an art film is the one in Gide's *Symphonie Pastorale* when the old person tries to bring in the blind, half-mad children from the snow to eat. This is done by tapping on the bowl with a spoon, in the icy, snowy winter. It has the effect of rendering *cold* better than I have ever seen it rendered in any film. I don't recall much of the rest of the picture.

The following wonderful passage in *Castle to Castle* of Céline: "The head is a kind of factory that doesn't run exactly the way you'd like . . . imagine . . . two thousand billion neurons . . . all a complete mystery . . . where does that get you?"

Céline is very lucky, even after death, to have visited upon his work the hell-raising translation of Ralph Manheim. Some people just get lucky, even those who have been collaborators with the Nazis.

American poets like Adrienne Rich are *all right*, but there is nothing particular in her work besides a kind of refinement of the current period style.

Take up with John Boorman his most recent additions to the script. Point out to him that we *must* preserve the cyclic nature of the story. He wants to get into the action *too* quickly. It would be much more effective if we had less river and more before-and-after life of the people involved, particularly that of Ed Gentry. I want very much for the audience to get to know him as a reasonably matter-of-fact husband and white-collar worker. It is not nearly as effective to have these things brought out in conversation. The old Broadway adage still holds: "Don't tell 'em; show 'em."

There are a great many writers who are good without having any particular talent. They deal with learnable entities.

Again, discontinuity. Most of the poets of my generation depend on this as if it were their very salvation. The trouble is, they try to "make it new" in ways that are very predictable and don't matter.

A good phrase from Stanley Kauffmann, characterizing John Osborne's *Look Back in Anger:* "one long whine."

Scene in the film of *Deliverance:* when Ed and Bobby are getting ready to go back to the city a car pulls up. It is an umarked car, just like anybody else's. It stops, and it is obvious that Ed and perhaps Bobby, as apprehensive as they are, figure that the car stopping has something to do with them. We go in slowly with the camera where there is this figure in the car in a cowboy hat or some kind of wide-brimmed hat, sitting completely in shadow, so that we don't know who it is. We *build* this moment. We go in closer with the camera very, very slowly, and then we get in close enough to see that it is the sheriff, with his blue eyes staring in hard, enigmatic fascination at the two city men. Has he found out everything? Does he know anything? Ed, uncertainly, goes over to the car. The sheriff says, rather slowly, but with that intonation that may mean everything or nothing, "Good morning."

Our time is a very sad and funny one in the realm of literary attack. One might call it the age of the moral put-down: if you don't side with me in being against the Vietnam war, then your poetry's no good.

This is a day of very great rejoicing for me: James Agee is a far better poet, in verse, than I thought him to be. Thank God. Thank God.

I was never really young, because my generation went into the war. I found my true youth in middle age, and it is much better than the actual youth that I had. It is good to think of this.

The first thing I mean to do when I get to Clayton this
Friday is to talk for a long time to John. I then need to
talk to the actors, get a sense of them and their
capacities, and then talk to John again. We need to have
a very long script conference, I need to see the
locations, and a lot of other things. It is going to be an
awfully hard-working summer, but I am really ready for
it, and will not give down. It is going to be one hell of
a film. I am very pleased that Jon Voight is going to
play Ed Gentry. Burt Reynolds, who is Lewis, I have
not seen work at all, but he looks and sounds good, for
he is a former stunt man, and that surely will come in
handy on the Chattooga River.

The new record of my readings has just come out and I
am very much interested in seeing it and hearing it. But
over the phone I talked to an executive at Caedmon
Records, and learned the terrible news that my little
namesake, Jamie Clark, died two weeks ago. I now have
only one child, Tuck, named after me, and I feel terribly
diminished. What's in a name, indeed.

Long restless nights. A new creative period is coming up;
I feel it, and I am ready.

It seems to me that most of the poets of my generation
are paying entirely too much attention to the topical. I
will utilize the topical to just the extent that it contains
things I sincerely want to write about, and no more. But
generally I am in search of something that transcends *all*
topicality, and transcends it easily. There are a great
many more important things than those that we read in
the newspapers every day. There is the sense of being a
human being alive on the planet. True, that human being
is alive among certain social and political and
environmental conditions, and these should be written
about, according to the temperament and wishes of the

writer in question. But we are universal as well as time-bound, and it is the universal that I am trying to connect with, in whatever way.

Another possible title for the Wesleyan address is "The Climate of Guilt."

The great curse of our time is overintellectualization. No one can get clear or make a decision, because it is possible to be cutely bright.

The bellwether of all intellectual cuteness and overintellectualization is Norman Mailer. What we need is simplicity, and not this kind of thing. It is a kind of substitute for literary talent, battening on current events. If there is anything the country needs less than that at this time I can't name it.

In *Death's Baby Machine*, have a report by Riker of a conversation that Riker has had with Joel Cahill. It has got around that Cahill has been talking to some of the other cadets in a way that Riker has come to think subversive. He has called him in and asked him about some of this. Riker says to the elder Cahill that "He had some kind of cracked-brain scheme, I think. He was trying to talk people out of going on as cadets, and even to refusing any order whatever." Cahill then asks him if Joel had any success with this, and Riker says, "Some, and I was, frankly, afraid he was going to have more. He was a very persuasive boy. Very strange, almost hypnotic, at least to some people. I'll be frank with you. I didn't really know what to make of him. I still don't." Cahill says, "Could you tell me a little bit more about him?" Riker says, "He was the best pilot in his class, and one of the two or three best that have been through here since I've been commandant. He could fly almost from the very first hour he was in the air better than most of the people we graduate from here. You only had to show him a thing one time, and he could not only do it, but improve on it. His instructor, Jack McCaig, was sold on him, and told me he used to look forward to every ride he gave Cahill. When I was talking to Joel, I told him he had a real future in the Air Force, and that he had all the qualifications for going on and making a career of it."

Then Cahill says, "What did he say to that?"

And Riker says, "He just kind of laughed at it. He said that would be the last thing on earth he would be interested in. He said that he didn't believe that men should fight, he didn't believe in machines, he didn't believe in wars, and he didn't believe in people being forced to do things—military things—that they didn't want to do or didn't believe in doing. I asked him what he did believe in, and he said freedom. I then told him, as nearly as I can remember, that men must sometimes fight to be free."

And Cahill says, "And he said?"

Riker says, "He said that that had been sold to the American public for such a long time that people believed it on a surface level, but that events showed that this was not true at all."

Cahill says, "What did you say then?"

And Riker says, "I told him that men always had to fight for their freedoms, and this had always been true, and always would be true. I asked him if he didn't believe that Hitler and Germany should be stopped. I asked him if he didn't believe that the war with Germany and Italy and Japan was absolutely necessary."

Cahill says, "And?"

"He replied that he was not by any means convinced of it. I then told him that in spite of his quality as a potential pilot, we could get rid of him quite easily on attitude, though we surely could not legitimately do so on his flying ability. I told him that if he didn't stop this senseless and adolescent subversiveness, I would do just that."

Cahill says, "How did he take it?"

Riker says, "He told me that he was not admitting to anything subversive at all. He then said that if he were doing something of the sort, he could carry on the work as well from radio school, gunnery school, mechanics school, or anywhere else he happened to end up. As long as he was alive, he said, he could go on with whatever work he wanted to, and there was nothing we could do about it. He said that if we imprisoned him, it would simply make his cause more effective, and that he could carry it on with equal or even greater effectiveness if he were given a dishonorable discharge and sent back to civilian life. I remember his saying that he could carry on any work he chose to as long as the U.S. mails still went to servicemen, and the APOs still existed."

Have, in the fragmentary writing of Joel Cahill, the phrase, "We'll give them a machine that *is* a machine! One that will smash theirs to pieces."

After the conversation with Riker, Cahill is more than ready to listen to the opinions of Harbelis and of McCaig, both of whom are convinced that Riker in his AT-6 forced Joel Cahill's plane over the fire, or perhaps even down into it, resulting in Cahill's death. After all, the three of them reason, Joel has already told Riker that as long as he lived he would likely be carrying on some kind of military subversion. It would then seem logical to these three that Riker killed him and made it look like an accident. This is why McCaig feels that he and Cahill should go over and talk to the farmer that pulled Joel Cahill out of the wreckage.

What emerges is that Joel Cahill did actually have some kind of subversion in mind, and it was not just talking to a few cadets, either. He has set down a timetable of revolt. He has a mimeographed letter, a couple of copies of which survive, which is to be sent to military personnel. Whether any of these have actually gone out, nobody knows. But he has a primitive chart of the echelons of men he is going to try to reach. The point is that Joel at least *intends* to bring about a general mutiny of military personnel, a strike, a walkout that will involve, ideally, everybody in the service, including those overseas. Graduating classes will refuse their commissions, other officers, or at least key officers, will turn their commissions in, enlisted men of all varieties will walk out, or refuse orders, and the MPs will refuse to arrest them. Joel wants the whole system to collapse. The timetable for this is his own graduation day when, presumably, he is supposed to get his commission on graduating from advanced flying school.

There are notes from the speech that Joel intends to make at his graduation: a call for brotherhood, and a sketchy outline of several paragraphs together with a few cryptic fragments, phrases, and so on. Some of these are simple adolescent statements—about what you would expect—but others are cryptic and tantalizing, sometimes metaphysical and Heraclitean, and odd in other ways. It should be fun to do these, or at least I hope so. The main thing is that Joel remains both explicable and completely inexplicable. What Cahill finds out about him only deepens the mystery. The difficulty here will be to make Joel as mysterious and enigmatic as I can.

About Joel's ground school grades. They were adequate.

In the conversation with Riker, also have Riker ask him, "Do you like flying?" And Joel answers, "No, not especially. I don't like machines. If I were going to have any attachment to flying at all, it would be to soaring, which has no military purpose, is slow, and has some aesthetic value." Riker then says to Joel, "Don't you know that the whole Luftwaffe came out of soaring?" Joel says, "That was only the use it was put to. I thought you were talking about the thing itself."

An important point about the character of Joel Cahill. He identifies with people. The post doctor can hint at this, or as much as he knows of it, anyway. But Joel identifies with people he admires, like Lawrence of Arabia, Napoleon, James Thomson, and a good many others, and there should be hints that he believes he can combine all these people in himself; poets, political leaders, generals, revolutionaries, and so on. Work this out in some detail, and leave the *proper* hints in the book. But hints, only.

The trouble with the work of the contemporary formalists like Thom Gunn and John Holloway is that their work contains too much conclusiveness and not enough strange inevitability. The emphasis here is on the word *strange*.

Joel's plan for revolution he calls "Operation Freeze-Out." This is found in a literature textbook that is among his effects, and has been appropriated by Harbelis as a kind of memento. The plan for Armed Forces mutiny is on three flyleaves in the back of the literature book. Some

of these are illegible, but others give a tantalizing idea of
his intentions. There are also a number of Heraclitean
aphorisms and other rather esoteric things. The last
word on the last of the three pages is *unlock*.

Also in the book are a number of underlined passages. It
is this that gives the elder Cahill the clue to what is
meant by the initials B.V. written on Joel's goggles,
which Frank Cahill carries in his pocket, and ends up
carrying for the rest of his life. B.V. are the initials taken
as a pen name by James Thomson, and stand for Bysshe
Vanolis, which latter is an anagram for Novalis, Bysshe
being Percy Shelley's middle name.

We might also want to cite lines in Thomson's poem "The
City of Dreadful Night," which have taken Joel Cahill's
fancy. Chief among these is "As I came through the
desert, thus it was."

In Joel Cahill's schema, there is apparently, also, some
kind of connection between poetry and revolt, and the
power of words in a certain order to move men to
action. It is not revealed as to which poems he intends
to use in his attack on the military establishment, but it
should be at least fairly apparent that he plans to use it
in *some* way, as yet and forever undisclosed. This could
account for some aphorisms having to do with action,
with poetry, with poetry-as-action, that Cahill finds in
the back of the literature book, which is just a standard
college text.

It also might be hinted in various ways, among them
these notebook entries and plans, that Joel plans to
reorganize the Armed Services in a way which might
include the free exercise of homosexuality, though
nowhere else is there any hint that he is or might be
homosexual. There might be some reference to Stefan

George's ideas about comradeship, and so on. It might be also hinted that Joel has ideas of becoming a very special kind of mystical fascist, though there is not enough material here to justify our assuming this as being absolutely true.

There is always a difficulty, in novels in which the main character never appears; is absent, dead, or whatever. But this is not an insuperable artistic problem; it is merely a very difficult one. When the reader finishes *Death's Baby Machine*, I want him to feel that he would really like to have known Joel Cahill: that the absence of Joel from the world of the living is just as acutely and tantalizingly felt by him—the reader—as it is by his father, Harbelis, Ellen, and the other people who have known him. I want the reader to search for Joel Cahill— for all the enigmatic Joel Cahills of this world—just as his father is doing in the novel.

Scene toward the end where Cahill, McCaig, and Riker are together in a kind of three-cornered confrontation. Riker says, "There's nothing anybody can ever prove, one way or the other, but if it's any satisfaction to you, I didn't do it, or anything like it." McCaig says, "The hell you didn't." All the time this dialogue is going on, the blind man, Cahill, whose dog is now dead, and is being kind of looked after by Harbelis, the Greek athlete, is standing between the two antagonists like a statue, saying nothing, and neither one of the antagonists knows which he believes.

The plan that Joel Cahill is working out, Operation Freeze-Out, must not only be interesting: it must be fascinating, in itself. That is, it must be some ingenious thing that might *work*.

As Joel Cahill is presented, he must also have something of the aspect of a Billy Budd, except that he is not beguiling and enigmatically good, but enigmatically evil, in some ways. This should come out in the elder Cahill's conversation with Ellen, who knows a good deal more about Joel than anyone else, and a lot of things about him that nobody else knows.

It should be great to work on Joel's notes for revolution. For example, in one place on his chart he has
Operation Freeze-Out   Operation Death-Baby   which?
    Start with cadets.
    Start with *one* cadet.
This could be the nucleus of the whole thing.

Have this plan, chart, notes, and the rest of it, described to the elder Cahill by Harbelis, and then reproduce it on the page as he goes through it. Then, perhaps, show the whole schema on three pages of the novel itself. This might work.

For some reason known only to him, Joel Cahill has given his father as next of kin. Perhaps the mother is dead; I haven't decided that yet. But most likely she is not, which makes Joel's naming of his father as next of kin have more point, more mystery.

In reference to this last entry, there could be part of a conversation between Harbelis or Ellen where Cahill tells this, and one of these could say, "Maybe he wanted you to come up here, if anything happened to him." Cahill says, "But how could he know that I would come, even if he was killed?" And the other says, "He would know. He was never wrong about things like that." And Cahill says, "I didn't even know him. I haven't seen him since he was a baby." The other says, "That wouldn't make any difference to him."

For the fragments and phrases and statements of Joel Cahill, study both the aphorisms of Heraclitus and those

of Kafka. I want something of the "this may mean
everything or nothing" quality of both of these writers
in the few things that Joel jots down. These would have
something to do with poetry, power, revolution, the
quality of life, brotherhood, peace, love, combat, conflict,
and other subjects: large subjects, always enigmatic. There
might also be references to subjects like poetry, love, art,
time—and especially, death. Also some things, maybe,
on the soul, immortality, and so on. Nikos Kazantzakis
might also be a case in point here, for he was another
one of these emotional, philosophical, enigmatic,
metaphysical, mysterious, will-prone types, as I want Joel
to seem to have been.

We now must work out a number of important relations,
particularly the relationship of the girl with Joel. I must
think about this a long time, because what Joel has
revealed to her will be most important. What will it be?
What was this—the emotional, sexual side—like?

In his interview with the post doctor, Cahill receives the
opinion that the doctor simply thought of Joel as a
rather eccentric but likable boy. He has treated him for a
couple of minor ailments, like seed-warts on the bottom
of his feet, for example, and has talked to him, and
has also been asked to talk to him some more by Riker,
which he does. Cahill asks him if he thinks Joel was
subversive or dangerous in any way, and the doctor says,
"Good God, no! He was just high-strung and intelligent,
and had a lot of ideas and enthusiasms."

Could there be a scene where Joel, surprisingly enough,
joins in with an instructor in beating up a fellow cadet?
What might this signify?

Pursuant to the last entry, the elder Cahill might ask
Harbelis, or another cadet who worshiped Joel, "Why

would he do that?" And the other would answer,
"Nobody ever knew. Nobody ever asked him. He just
did it. There was no telling what he would do. Nobody
questioned him, except the military. Nobody in the corps
ever did. He just did what he wanted to."

It would appear from the things that the elder Cahill
hears about Joel that he acted according to a mysterious,
ritualistic manner of his own. To other people, these were
strange, eccentric actions, and it is only as we go through
the novel that we become aware that there is a secret
pattern to them, although we never find it out
completely.

The self-creation of figures like T. E. Lawrence is an
obvious parallel here. Reread the section of the *Seven
Pillars* where Lawrence reasons out his plan of attack, his
concept of guerrilla warfare against the Turks. Perhaps
something of this can be applied to Joel's scheme of
subverting the entire American Armed Forces.

I think we are all talking ourselves to death, me
included.

Dialogue, on the part of Harbelis or somebody else in the
cadets: "You don't come on somebody like him but once
or twice in a lifetime. No; once."

Are there any plans that Cahill might have, or hint at,
for what he intends to do after his "take-over"? There
might be some hint or other, but these would have to go
in one of two ways. The first would be toward some
kind of brotherhood, and the second would be toward
the acquisition of some sort of power by himself, or by
an elite headed by himself.

Pursuant to the last entry, it seems to me that Joel might
hint at some "new order," and this would be

characterized by some very weird but imaginative ideas about how men should live on this earth, and about how society should function. Of course we cannot have a whole textbook on this, but if possible we should hold out some hints to the reader.

I want Joel to "solve" all the things that the "now" generation of revolutionaries has not been able to solve. They can offer only unlimited sex, drugs, free stores, people's parks, and other unimaginative solutions. Joel would offer something entirely different, and I must figure out what this might be, or what he might have thought it to be.

I think Joel's new order would have to be ritualistic and symbolic in some way. What way?

For example, in the original version of *Deliverance*, I had Lewis talk at great length about a new society of "Survivors," who would turn their backs on machinery and roam the forests as nomads, hunting with bows and arrows, fishing, accompanied by their minstrels, with guitars and dulcimers. Of course, nothing of this sort could be used by Joel, but there should be a strange kind of inventiveness in his conception of his new society, which, as he says, begins by convincing one cadet so that he will *act*.

Now comes the problem: how has Riker come, if he has, to believe that he should kill Joel Cahill? If he has done this, it might be simply because he dislikes him, which is hardly motivation enough, or because of his adverse effect on the cadet corps, plus his conversation with Joel about Joel's being subversive at any level, even the civilian level. But I would also like to hint that Riker had got an inkling, some slight notion, of the enormity of Joel's plan, and had been frightened terribly by it. I don't

know how this information could be got to Riker, for
he obviously doesn't read literary textbooks, which is
where the plan is outlined as much as it ever turned
out to be outlined. But it could come through somebody,
and it could come in one statement. Could it be Ellen,
Harbelis, some other cadet: the cadet colonel, perhaps?
I'm not sure, here. But I would like some indication to be
given to the reader that Riker has really been shaken by
the harm, as he understands it, that might be done by
such an individual, particularly by one whom the other
boys worship! who can also do everything the system
asks him to do, easily and with a certain amount of
contempt.

We do not want to paint Riker as a superpatriot, a right-
winger, or anything else of that sort. He is merely
"there's a war on" type. Joel might have something to
say about this in his notes, or in a remembered
conversation with one of the cadets. Joel is, if not exactly
a master of the phrase, at least a master of it to the
extent that his compatriots remember what he says. He
may have had a particular characterizing epithet for
Riker that has caught on with the boys and that had got
back to Riker in some manner, as such things always do.

I am slightly dubious about the film possibilities of
Death's Baby Machine, particularly because so much of
the story pertains to a character who is never seen. Some
of the scenes could be very effective, but the justification
for the film—as, indeed, for the novel—will have to be
the interaction between the living people we can see,
rather than the dead boy that we never see.

One of the points here is that Cahill is a relatively
ordinary man, and has had nothing whatever to do with
political thought, revolutions, or anything of that sort. He
just wants to run his swimming pool and skating rink,

and go along with the rest; the society does pretty well by him, and he is grateful enough, in his way. Now that his own son is revealed to him, slowly, bit by bit, conversation by conversation, he is not so sure of where he stands. The point here is to show the slow awakening of a complacent and seriously maimed ordinary man toward political and social realities, and to the fire, or at least the flicker, of genius: to the disruptive effect that one individual may have on a society, and the change that it might bring about, even though, in this case, the change never occurs, and was probably foredoomed. What Joel comes to represent to his father, however, is the play of the mind on these subjects and the importance of them.

Joel says, in one of his notes, "We are righter than they are. I know it. I can see them, but they can't see me."

Who is his "we"? So far, there is only Joel, and, in an embryonic way, Harbelis. Is this delusion, or is something really dangerous getting started here in this obscure village in North Carolina? We never know that, but the audience should be convinced that Joel Cahill, young as he is, might just possibly have hold of something. Something big as an idea, though he probably could not— almost certainly—ever have carried it out. That's the point: the *idea* here. We must work this out in detail so that the idea that Joel has will ramify in the minds of the readers.

I don't want to make Joel Cahill yet another Jerry Rubin-like student revolutionary in uniform. I want him to be seen as a real adolescent seer, although only fragmentarily one.

Also as part of this story, I think it very important indeed that we get an increasing sense of the way the elder Cahill, some of the time consciously and at other times unconsciously, begins to get a sharpening of the senses of touch and hearing. We should have him make observations of rooms, of people, of voices, of the way people's hands feel, of the way fabrics feel, hard objects like tables and stones feel, and so on. Toward the end, there is even a sense in which he has a bat-like sense of "radar" by which he measures echoes, reverberations, and so on. This should hint at the fact that, with luck, and with the right situation, he has the chance of becoming a more remarkable blind man than he ever was as a sighted man. Let his mind awaken a little, too, under the stimulus of Joel's.

Maybe there is a scene where Cahill and McCaig, Joel's instructor, get drunk together, and the elder Cahill, overcome with what he has discovered and longing for his boy that he has never known, simply stands up and screams out Joel's name. McCaig calms him down and they sit down in this joint where they are, and McCaig says, "Well, he can't hear you. He's somewhere out there in the dark." And Cahill says very quietly, looking in the direction of McCaig's voice, "Yes, he is. But he may hear me."

Also the scene where the elder Cahill says to somebody —Harbelis, McCaig, Ellen, or maybe even Riker—"I've never loved anybody in my life. But I love him."

Also, maybe in connection with the latter conversation, he can say, "He was my son. No; he *is* my son."

The basic problem of this novel is to create a character of potentially major dimensions who is never seen, but who is projected by means of his posthumous effect on other people, and whose implications, insofar as they may be known at all, come to rest in his blind father. This is a terribly difficult undertaking, and must be thought out slowly and in hundreds of details.

The novel also should pass, insofar as the elder Cahill is concerned, from an interest, which any father would have, in what a son he had never known was like, to a kind of obsession with the boy, or at least a fascination with him. There might even be a suggestion that he will go to see the boy's mother, and will have photographs described, and letters read to him. He himself has never received one word from the boy, and he will be acutely aware of this in his dealings with others who have had more contact with Joel.

I don't want Joel Cahill to be one of those dreadful philosophizing journal-keepers, such as the doctor in Walker Percy's *The Last Gentleman*. No; the stuff must be very fragmentary indeed, nothing spelled out, but only hinted, but the hints must be both tantalizing and luminous. And that is going to be tough; very tough.

Perhaps there is a scene where McCaig flies the elder Cahill, in the open trainer, over the place where Joel went down. Of course there is no fire now, but McCaig yells back through the gosport, "It was right in here somewhere," as though he were talking to someone who could see. Later, when the elder Cahill says goodbye to McCaig, he refers to this. He says, "I hope you will keep in touch with me, some way or the other, no matter what you happen to wind up doing." McCaig says, "Well, sure I will. But why do you want me to?" And Cahill answers, "Because you flew me over the place where my boy died. I couldn't see it, and you knew that, but you never asked me why I wanted to go there. That's enough for me."

I must include, also, a relatively long section about Cahill's oncoming blindness, his visits to opticians, doctors,

and so on. There should be something on his final
realization of the *dawning* of blindness, when he is
totally out of the world of sight, and a similar section
concerning his rehabilitation, his going through a clinic
for the blind in the middle of the war, when there are
few technicians and rehabilitation people to help him, his
acquisition of a seeing-eye dog, how this encounter takes
place, and so on. All this can be poignant and moving,
and should take twenty or thirty pages, or maybe not
quite that much. Anyway, it should do everything that
needs to be done about establishing the mental condition
of a man who has *gone* blind in middle age.

There must also be this enormous yearning-back to the
world of visual images, so that the mental images of the
world that he has seen become incandescent in Cahill's
mind. One of these might be the image of the girl
through the one-way mirror at his swimming pool
establishment. Of that girl, a gum-chewing, little high
school cheerleader type, he will be able, or think himself
able, to remember every goose pimple on her thighs. This
will be sort of like his vision of the lost paradise. He
dwells on this all the time: it is his entire sexual world,
and the connection that we all deserve to have between
the visual and the sexual. That is gone for him, now. It
all must go into touch, and, yes, into hearing.

The most dangerous tendency that we have to resist in
this novel—as is true of any artistic work—is what I might
call the lock-in tendency: the tendency to perpetuate one's
first conception, to spend a lot of time writing *into*
that first conception when the conception itself might be
totally wrong. In this case, I don't want to have to
unwrite a lot of stuff because the initial conception was
wrong to begin with. That is why we have to think the
whole thing through very carefully. I did this with
Deliverance, and most of the critics, as a result, talk about
how well it is plotted. That is true; in *Deliverance*, one

thing follows from another; the novel has that sense of inevitability that I want this one to have. But *Death's Baby Machine* is enormously more complicated than *Deliverance*, which, after all, is a straightforward adventure story. This one is a difficult technical undertaking, and I must be sure I have exactly what I want before I begin to write the scenes and fill in the details.

I think one of the very best openings for a novel that I have ever read is the beginning of Richard Hughes' *Fox in the Attic*.

In *Death's Baby Machine* I think it is a very good instinct to open with the elder Cahill in the wayside rooming house, awakened by the wind. He opens his eyes, and there is no difference. He panics, and then he calls for Zack, and he can hear the foot-clicks of the beast coming across the floor to him. He lies back in the eiderdown quilts and feels for Zack's head, and it comes into his hand. He can hear the breathing of the animal. This is his eyes.

He felt in the dark; he held out his hand, and something came into it. He should feel along Zack's lips, feel his teeth, and, very gently, his eyes. He should run his hand along Zack's side, along the thick fur. He should pat Zack's side and tell him to lie down. Then he asks Zack to get up on the bed, and Zack does not understand. He asks again and Zack still does not understand, and then Cahill asks him to lie on the floor, says get down, or whatever term he has learned in the school for the blind, and he feels the animal sink away beneath his hand, though he can still hear him breathe.

After this first awakening to the wind, without the reader's knowing exactly what is going on, and why Cahill can't see, we should simply have a short paragraph: "Zack," he said softly.

The first thing that we must keep in the foreground of
our mind about Joel is that he is a creative, even if crazy,
dreamer; he is not just someone who, if he lived in our
time, would be wandering around in a chemically-induced
trance. He has *ideas*, and it will be up to me to find them.
These *must* be crazy and provocative. They must center
on revolution, but they must also seem to hint that some
entirely *different* order of being might be instituted for
men, if someone could think of it. He is engaged, in a
kind of adolescent and yet shrewd and imaginative way, in
thinking of it. Working this out is going to be tough, but
will also be a good deal of fun. Maybe, in trying to
imagine Joel's thinking of it, *I* can think of it: can think
of the thing to change the whole picture, and the way
people take each other's and their life on earth. Where
would technology fit into this, for example?

In Chris I have produced a son who can *think*.

I just happened on an extraordinarily relevant—relevant to
the film version of *Deliverance*—sentence and concept in
Stanley Kauffmann. He is talking about *Easy Rider*, and he
says, "it tries to explore its subject, to throw its characters
into it, and let them take their chances . . ." If that
is not what we are trying to do with the film of
Deliverance, I don't know *what* we are trying to do.
And, parenthetically, the characters—and actors—are taking
a lot more chances, literal chances, in *Deliverance* than
they ever did in *Easy Rider*. Of course that does not
mean that *Deliverance* will be a better film, though I am
absolutely convinced that it will be. But it simply means
that if you throw your characters into an action and have
them take their chances, the "chances" can be seen as
possible triumphs and disasters beyond the merely artistic.
The actors in *Deliverance* are risking their lives, and this
is fact. I have seen them going over those falls, and
nothing in *Easy Rider* approximated this in danger.

Perhaps danger—actual physical danger to the actors—has nothing whatever to do with the aesthetic import of a film. Again, perhaps it does.

Can there be some things in Joel's remarks about kingship, sun worship, and things of that nature? The notion of the mystical import of leadership should come in here somewhere, and it should be, in an adolescent way, intellectually respectable. Question is, is Joel to be seen as a liberator, or a new enslaver? Or, even more important, the architect of a new liberation-through-enslavement? Or, even more to the point, the architect of a new enslavement-through-liberation?

Or maybe we shouldn't make Joel so grandiose a revolutionary, but simply have him recalcitrant and uncooperative. How would this serve? I was much taken with the other idea, but now I see how it might be said that I attempted to cash in on the youth rebellion with a species of hindsight, and attempted to translate the whole thing back to 1942. Nevertheless, there does have to be something deeply disturbing to people about Joel Cahill, and it *must* have something to do with subverting the system. There are lots of ways to do this, and I must try to find the right one.

All right. Let's try it this way. To the different people who have known him, Joel Cahill seems to be different people. The post doctor sees him as an intelligent, impetuous, and imaginative kid. Ellen sees him another way. McCaig sees him as a real man, one who won't take any shit off of 'em. Riker's mistress sees him another way, perhaps simply as a fabulous stud. Harbelis sees him as a kind of military saint, and the other cadets see him as a superior performer who is his own man. The one Joel really *frightens* is Riker, and this fully as much because of what Riker is as because of what Joel represents to him.

For example: suppose Riker sends Joel on to basic, which he must do unless he can kick him out for "attitude." And suppose that, in basic, Joel foments real revolt among the cadets? What then, for Riker? For Groome, the Army check-rider, he represents yet another problem: someone who can, with just a few hours of flying, outdo anything that Groome can do. People know this, and this is embarrassing for Groome, who has already washed out a couple of combat-type aircraft and thus has been relegated to the inferior status of Army check-rider in a primary training school. The point is that Joel represents all these different things to these different people. But, I repeat, the only one that he really *frightens* is Riker. This is because Riker himself is an insecure, petit bourgeois type completely dependent on the military to underprop him, and also because he is the kind of man who is able to persuade himself that getting rid of adverse elements like Joel constitutes a kind of patriotic or civic duty. There are lots of these people around, but there is nowhere in American society in which it is more possible to take the law into one's own hands than the military, and this is particularly true of the wartime military. We must play up this aspect of Riker's personality in subtle ways: the self-justification, the self-aggrandizement. That is the greatest peril to society coming from people in authority, and it is nowhere more completely crystallized or manifest than in the military, particularly in the higher officers and middle officers.

We must now work out the character of Ellen—if that is what I end up calling her—in detail: where she comes from, what her life has been like, how she met Joel, and so on. We must go into her medical history, not at length, but convincingly, in a few details.

It may be, even in these early stages, that *Death's Baby Machine* is foredoomed to failure. Even so, even if I cannot realize the character of Joel as I wish to do, some of the scenes will save it, I am quite sure. I *know* I can write the scenes, though I don't know, frankly, whether I can bring the whole thing off as a novel. I believe that it can be done, but I don't know whether or not *I* can do it. Well, here goes.

Remark by Ellen at the end, when Cahill asks her what he looks like. She says, "Well, your skin is getting to look kind of shot."

There might be some kind of value in having Ellen speak Air Force jargon. That is, if I can remember enough of it.

In *everything,* beware of the lock-in syndrome. There is that in a writer which makes him carry out his original conception no matter what. I have not been guilty of this as much as some have, but I have been plenty guilty, nevertheless. The trouble is that so many things of value are conceived of in trying to carry through a scheme that would never have worked in the first place. That can't be the case with this novel: I must get the general scheme I want, and *then* carry it through, and I must be convinced—not convince myself, which is quite a different thing—that this is the right structure for the book.

As I see her now, Ellen is rather a lighthearted dying girl. And the scene in which she relates her medical misfortunes can be hilarious, as well as harrowing. This should take up maybe two or three paragraphs, but they should be good ones. I must find out more about leukemia, its onset, and the rest. Or maybe that's not what the matter with her is. But whatever it is, it must include heavy, periodic, and unexpected nosebleeds. There is no one on earth sicker-looking than someone with a nosebleed. It is unexplicable, because most noses don't bleed, or at least most of the time. So—consult with Don Saunders about this, and take his advice, meanwhile exploring some of the other symptoms of the particular disease that would cause this.

Cahill is constantly *interpreting* things: that is, the way he thinks they might look or, even, *must* look. Sometimes we get contrasts between what he thinks he sees—that is, images in his mind that have come from images when he could see—and what is actually around him or before him. One of the things he thinks he can do is imagine the way people look from the way they speak and the way they feel. This is what should give the final scene with the girl, on the last page, a special kind of poignancy, for he finally admits to himself that he cannot do this, and will probably never be able to. When he asks her what she looks like, and asks her to tell him what he looks like, it should be a moment of very special effect.

Part of Joel's "take-over plan" might be a kind of sketchy table of organization. This would indicate that he is only going to set up another kind of bureaucracy— albeit determinedly "idealistic"—for the one we already have. Don't come down too hard on the irony of this, but make it implicit to the observant reader.

Strange business, this confession of Jason Epstein under the direction of J. Edgar Hoover. I found Epstein's words very moving and hope very much that he uttered them sincerely. However, I am sure there is a great deal of speculation about his being brainwashed by Hoover and the FBI, since he has just emerged from a month in their dungeons. How was it that J. Edgar Hoover got this militant leftist intellectual to recant and repent so thoroughly under these particular conditions? I wish I knew. But the fact is, I believe Epstein when he says what he does.

The real brainwashing in cases like Epstein's has been the brainwashing of the herd-instinct New York intellectuals. You can't really be "in" up there unless you are with them on their stand against the Vietnam war and virulently anti-American. As Epstein says, this is plainly a case of using anti-Americanism as a form of ego-upmanship: "I am more moral than you since you don't share my viewpoint." Surely this is the age of moral blackmail, and Epstein's statement, no matter how elicited, brings this out about as well as it could be brought out.

Don't you know the *New York Review of Books'* intellectuals are in a flap because of Epstein's statement! How the conversation must be going in that sector tonight! What talk of brainwashings! What talk of sellouts! What talk, what talk, what talk! And how the *New York Review of Books* is going to capitalize on this, publishing feature articles, refutations, letters to the editor, and so on! God deliver me, and somehow I think He will.

One thing Ellen might say to the elder Cahill about Joel's sexual life is that "I played to his fantasies. He said that before he met me the only sexual life he ever had was to put something up his ass and jack off."

But what were the fantasies? This might provide some very rare-type stuff, here! Also very revelatory.

Our poor dog, Thunderball, bred as an Australian sheep-working dog, now doomed to pass his life chasing garbage trucks, trying to herd other neighborhood dogs into a ring, chasing mailmen, speedboats, and other phantoms.

George C. Scott could play Frank Cahill, and very well too. I have seen him act roles in dark glasses and he looks authentically blind; very blind indeed.

In Ellen's recounting of her medical ills and diagnoses, let
there be something of the sick person's deliberate levity,
as though this serves as a kind of charm against the
disease itself.

Joel says to Ellen, "I've tried it with other girls, but they
couldn't get into my place with me. What I mean is, the
place where I really *live*." But what was this place? Joel's
fantasies are going to be a great deal of the key to
him, and will also give us room for some fantastic writing,
for Ellen is an imaginative girl, and what she cannot
remember of what Joel said, she can embroider herself,
for she has entered wholeheartedly into the complicity of
Joel's fantasies, and is even a good deal more articulate
than he is. But she is articulate in a country way, so that
her recounting of his stories and fantasies partakes of, in a
very strong sense, this "country surrealism" that I am
trying to get into some of the poems I write. I don't
wish her to do this in dialect, but the writing should be
very much in the colloquial, without being mannered. In
other words, it should be written plainly, as to diction,
but not as to imagination, and it should retain the flavor
of small-town and Southern country life without seeming
to be self-conscious about it.

What Joel does, if even in a very fragmentary, adolescent
way, is to get down to the very roots of things, as today's
radicals are trying to do, except that he is a great deal
more perceptive and penetrating than they are. He asks
unanswerable questions, questions concerning ethics, the
bases for action, altruism, all the ancient philosophical
questions. Although he fancies himself well-read, he is
really not bookish, but reasons from a relatively primitive
and relatively adolescent position. Nevertheless, the
questions should be very disturbing ones, even for an
adolescent. But this must *not* seem like a predating of
today's young militants, radicals, and so on. Joel might
very well have *been* an adolescent revolutionary visionary.

He says that the whole thing can begin by talking to, by convincing one cadet; so far that is all he has done. The rest is theory and grandiose plans, such as are made by boys. But they must be made to seem particularly peculiar and disturbing plans. Joel, ultimately, is going to be based on my son, Chris.

There should be, at least in one or two minds, a very real notion of martyrdom in Joel Cahill's death. Chief among these is Harbelis. Ellen did not look on him in this way, but shared his dialogues and his fantasies, and came to like, even to love him. Riker fears him, and is impressed by him. Frank Cahill himself does not know, at the end of the novel, exactly what to think, or how to take the son he has never seen. But he will not forget him, and he will be searching *himself*, for the rest of his life, for the clues to Joel's life, behavior, and death.

Some of the remarks by Joel's classmates, classmates from whom Cahill had hoped to get the most revelatory statements, are banal and very commonplace, like "He was a good ping-pong player. Not the best, but very good." Likewise, some of the most revealing statements come from people that Cahill has not been referred to, and would therefore not expect to have revealing statements come from.

There's now the character of Riker's mistress. Who is she? She is a girl who works on the base, in some kind of secretarial or at least office capacity. Beyond that, I have not begun to think much about her, except about her existence and her relatively minor but also important place in the general puzzle of the novel.

Could she work, for example, in equipment? This is one of those bases manned and staffed largely by civilians and run by the military. There are civilian instructors, civilian mechanics, civilian employees, and military overseers for the cadets. The cadets are instructed in flying by civilians, and in ground school by civilians, checked periodically by military personnel in the air, supervised by military personnel in drill formations and in physical training, and in all things are expected to answer, in the final analysis, to the military. Yet the field is predominantly civilian-dominated. This is one of the sources of friction between McCaig, a fine pilot from the old crop-duster days, and Riker, a commonplace military pilot with overhead connections. McCaig is essentially contemptuous of Riker, and he detests the military. Conversely, he loves Joel Cahill, whom he looks on as a kind of younger brother. For example, once McCaig has his pay docked and Joel has to walk a certain number of penalty tours as a result of their having gone up in an aircraft and "wrung it out." McCaig could have a good deal to say about this, about the technical names of the maneuvers they have done, and attempt to explain these to Cahill by taking Cahill's hand and waving it through the air in a pattern which he hopes Cahill will understand.

There is also the matter of the one cross-country that Joel took, along with two others of McCaig's instructees. McCaig can say that when Joel led the flight of three back, and came into the pattern first to land his aircraft while the others circled to land behind him, Joel managed to convey the impression that he was coming back into a torn-up airfield in England during the Battle of Britain. "There was that excitement about him," McCaig says. "The same thing was true when he was the first in his class to solo. There is always that excitement when someone is first to solo, but I have never seen, in two years on this field, and a good many classes, excitement like there was when Joel soloed. The whole class knew he was going to make them look good, and if Joel could do it, and do it as they knew he *would* do it, they would *all* be able to do it. And almost all of them have. All of them would graduate and go on to basic. And almost all of them are going to. All but him."

McCaig says, "I remember when he came out to the airplane to solo. Boy, he looked like Eddie Rickenbacker! He had a long ribbon on the back of his helmet, which was, you know, not *allowed*, but *kind of* allowed to the first man to try it. And I thought, 'That's my boy.' He walked right by me, and he said, 'Coach, you've made me.' I wish I had said back—I didn't, but I wish I had —'No, son, I didn't make you. You made me.'"

Question of the combat pilots, former cadets in primary school at this particular base, who visit the base. McCaig and Cahill take them out to drink beer. They run down Groome, Riker, and the others, who are officer "washouts." McCaig agrees with this, and they talk flying a little bit. Finally it comes out that Cahill's boy has been killed there; the first cadet ever killed in the school. The combat pilots are incredulous, though they recount escapes that they had, when engines cut out, they almost ran into each other, and one thing and another. Still, they cannot understand someone being *killed* in primary, and there is some back and forth conversation about this with McCaig mainly dominating the conversation.

Combat pilot—from Africa—and his story about the expansion of gas in the intestines as these new, fast planes like the P-38 and P-51 climb rapidly.

Scene beside the frozen-over swimming pool. The sound of ping-pong balls is heard in the background. Zack whines uneasily. Cahill and whoever he is talking to are sitting in those old board chairs beside the pool, and far away there is the noise of aircraft warming up, and overhead there is also the sound of 220 horsepower engines. There is the sound of their going into a maneuver, something like a barrel roll or a slow roll or a snap roll, and Cahill asks what causes the variation in the sound. The cadet, or whoever is with him, explains.

The whole question of *maps* in relation to Cahill. A good deal of the talk is about maps, and all of this has to be patiently explained to him. But he is with people who will explain patiently, if it takes forever, for he is Joel Cahill's father, and they feel that it is important for him to know. For him to know *everything*.

PART II

New Essays

THE SELF AS AGENT

Every poem written—and particularly those which make use of a figure designated in the poem as "I"—is both an exploration and an invention of identity. Because the poem is not the actual world of tactile sensations and relations, but must be represented as such by the agreed-upon meanings and the privately symbolic values of words, the person who is so identified often bears only a questionable and fugitive resemblance to the poet who sits outside the poem, not so much putting his I-figure through an action but attempting to find out what the I-figure will do, under these circumstances as they develop and round themselves out. The poem is admittedly a fiction; its properties are all fictional even if they are based on fact, and its devices are those of consciously manipulated artifice. The poem is created by what is said in it, and the *persona* of the I-figure is correspondingly conditioned far more by the demands of the poem as a formal linguistic structure than by those of the literal incident upon which it may be based. Therefore the notion of a poem-self identifiable with the author's real one, and consistent from poem to poem, is a misreading of the possibilities of poetic composition.

What is the motive on the part of the poet, in this regard? Why does he assign to "himself," as he appears in his own poems, such and such traits, such and such actions? In other words, why does he make himself act the way he does in his poems? This question could of course be answered in the most obvious way, by saying that there is bound to be some degree of wish-fulfillment present in the poet's practice, and undoubtedly there would be truth in the assertion. But more important than that, the I-figure's actions and meanings, and indeed his very being, are determined by the poet's rational or instinctive grasp of the dramatic possibilities in the scene or situation into which he has placed himself as one of the elements. To put it another way, he sees the creative possibilities of the lie. He comes to understand that he is not after the "truth" at all but something that he considers better. He understands that he is not trying to tell the truth but to *make* it, so that the vision of the poem will impose itself on the reader as more memorable and value-laden than the actuality it is taken from. In the work of many a poet, therefore, the most significant creation of the poet is his fictional self. The identity that is created by the devices and procedures of the poem has made him into an agent fitted more or less well, more or less perfectly, to the realm of the poem. The personality that the I-figure has therein may never recur, and the external poet, the writing poet, is under no obligation to make him do so. Likewise the *author's* personality as it changes from poem to poem is not itself assignable to any single poem. A certain Protean quality is one of the poet's most valuable assets. Therefore he is almost invariably embarrassed at the question he is bound to be asked about his poems: "Did you really *do* that?" He can only ask in turn: "Did *who* do it?"

From poem to poem the invented self is metamorphosed into whatever it is to become in the poem. Though language itself is the condition that makes the poem possible, there are a great number of other factors that make this particular *use* of language possible and, with luck, desirable. To use an analogy, the poem is a kind of local weather, and what creates it is the light that words in certain conjunctions play upon each other. It is a place of delicate shades as well as of sudden blindnesses, and, while it is in the process of being made, it is impossible for its creator to tell what the total light of the completed poem will be like. But no matter whatever else it may be likened to, the poem is a realm that is being created around the I-figure as he is being created within it. The poet knows that his figure will be taken for him; he knows that "this is supposed to be me," but the conditions by which he is limited and delimited in the poem are, in fact, nothing like the same ones that shape his actual life. During the writing of the poem, the poet comes to feel that he is releasing into its proper field of response a portion of himself that he has never really understood.

As for the I-figure himself, he is at first nebulous, ectoplasmic, wavering in and out of several different kinds of possible identity. He is a stranger in a half-chaotic place that may with fortune and time become familiar. Though by the time the poem is completed he may have become solid, dominant, and even godlike, he is tentative indeed at the beginning of the poet's labors. The poet in his turn exercises an expectant vigilance, always ready to do what the agent-self inside the poem requests him to; he will do what he can to make his agent act, if not convincingly, then at least dramatically, tellingly, memorably. The questions he must answer in this respect come to the poet in forms not so much like "What did I do then?" but rather "What might I have done?" or "What would it be interesting for me to do, given the situation as I am giving it?" Or perhaps, if the poet is prone to speak in this way, "What can I make my agent do that will truly *find* the poem: that will focus it on or around a human action and deliver a sense of finality and consequence, and maybe even that aura of strangeness that Bacon said every 'excellent beauty' must possess?"

As we know, it is part of the way in which the human being makes identifications to take the *persona* of the poem for the poet himself: to make him personally accountable not only for the poem's form and its insights but for the events which the poem describes, translated back into the world of real human beings and non-mental objects. Who does not, for example, identify Prufrock as Eliot? It is hard not to do this, even when the I-figure is designated in the title or by other means as a *persona*, as in Browning's "The Bishop Orders His Tomb at Saint Praxed's Church." In reflecting on such matters, one realizes the implications, both artistic and personal, that reside in Proust's injunction to Gide to the effect that one can "say anything, so long as one doesn't say 'I.'"

II

What does the poet begin with in attempting to create a personage in a poem who will bear the name "I"? With an individual in a time and at a place, or reflecting in a kind of timeless and placeless mental limbo. The poet usually gives him some overt or implied reason for speaking, and for reacting in a certain way to the events in which he finds himself or those that he thinks about. What he reacts to, for example, may be a condition or a person he knows well, or one he knows to some degree, or it may be something that acts upon him with the wonderful or uncertain or dreadful shock of newness. Now the poet believes that he understands his *persona* only to the extent that he understands himself. But that is not quite the case. For some unfathomable reason, the poet may find his "self" acting in quite an inexplicable way, often doing things that the poet never knew either of them knew. So the poem becomes not so much a matter of the poet's employing a familiar kind of understanding but rather a matter of aesthetic and personal curiosity: the placing of a part of himself into certain conditions to see what will come of it in terms of the kind of interaction between personality and situation he has envisioned from the beginning. He must of course then empathize, he must think himself into the character, but he must realize that his character also possesses the power to think itself into him and to some extent to dictate what he writes. For the poet's part, one of the most interesting things to note is that the poet is just as likely to attribute to his character traits that are diametrically opposed to those that the poet displays during his day-to-day existence. For this reason as well as for others, it is possible for psychologists to make a very great deal out of poems, as Ernest Jones does with *Hamlet,* to take one of the most obvious cases. But the poem, though it may be useful or instructive in this way, does not exist exclusively or even primarily for this reason, as we know. It is not because of its psychologically revelatory qualities that the poem interests us; it is its capacity to release to us—and release us to—insights that we otherwise assuredly would not have, giving these by means of the peculiar and inimitable formal devices of a practiced art.

As a poet, I have done a good deal of speculating on the kinds of ways certain poets might be presumed to make themselves think, act, and speak in their poems. And in my own work I have wrestled with the problem in my own way. For example, should the poet cause his I-figure to speak in a manner in which he might be expected to speak, but which *feels* wrong to the poet? And are the advantages and perils of first-person narration the same for poems as they are for novels and stories? Some of the best of our fiction writers—Henry James comes to mind—have called the first-person device a limited and even "barbarous" method. But for poetry as well as for fiction it has one quite simply incomparable characteristic, and that is credibility. When the poet says "I" to us—or, as Whitman does, "I was the man, I suffer'd, I was there"—we must either believe him completely or tell him in effect that he's a damned liar if his poem betrays him, by reason of one kind of failure or another, into presenting himself as a character in whom we either cannot or do not wish to believe. Because of its seeming verisimilitude, some recent writers have so overused the first person that they are designated—and rightly—as "confessional." And, though all poetry is in a sense confessional, no really good poetry is ever completely so, for "confessing" means "telling the truth and nothing but the truth," and, setting aside the question of whether that is really possible to any creature lower than the angels, it is evident that for any imaginative poet there are too many good opportunities outside of and beyond the mere facts to pass up; in most instances these are the opportunities that, when utilized and realized in the poem, make it more telling dramatically—and "truthful" as well. What the poet wishes to discover or invent is a way of depicting an action in a manner that will give at the same time the illusion of a truth-beyond-truth and the sense of a unique imaginative vision. The real poet invariably opts for the truth of the poem as against the truth of fact, the truth of truth.

And so the poet is aware, more than he is aware of anything else, of the expressive possibilities of his use of himself: that agent in the poem whom he calls "I." He feels a strange freedom and a new set of restrictions when he realizes that he can call into play—can energize—any aspect of himself he wishes to, even if he doesn't yet know what it is to be: any self that the poem calls for. He exults in his "negative capability" and can, as Keats says, take as much delight in creating an Iago as an Imogen. His personality is fluid and becomes what it is most poetically profitable for it to become, in the specific poem in which it comes to exist. Poems are points in time when the I-figure congeals and takes on a definite identity and ascertainable qualities, and the poet is able to appear, for the space of the poem, as a coherent and stabilizing part of the presentation, observing, acting, and serving as a nucleus of the unities and means and revelations of the poem, a kind of living focal point— or perhaps it would be better to say that he finds himself *living* the focal point. The better the poet is—Shakespeare, Browning—the more mercurial he will be, and, paradoxically, the more convincing each of his *personae* will be, for he can commit himself to each independently and, as it were, completely. The better the poet is, the more personalities he will have, and the more surely he will find the right forms to give each of them its being, its time and place, and its voice. A true poet can write with utter convincingness about "his" career as a sex murderer, and then in the next poem with equal conviction about tenderness and children and self-sacrifice. As Keats says, it is simply that the poet "has no personality." I would say, rather, that he has a personality large enough to encompass and explore each of the separate, sometimes related, sometimes unrelated, personalities that inhabit him, as they inhabit us all. He is capable of inventing or of bringing to light out of himself a very large number of I-figures to serve in different poems, none of them obligated to act in conformity with the others.

To speak personally, this has always seemed to me to constitute the chief glory and excitement of writing poetry: that the activity gives the poet a chance to confront and dramatize parts of himself that otherwise would not have surfaced. The poem is a window opening not on truth but on possibility: on the possibility for dramatic expression that may well come to *be* what we think of as truth, but not truth suffering the deadening inertia of what we regard as "actuality," but flowing with energy, meaning, and human feeling. I am quite sure that I myself, for example, owe to the activity of writing poetry my growing conviction that truth is not at all a passive entity, merely lying around somewhere waiting to be found out. I conceive it as something that changes in accordance with the way in which it is seen and more especially with the way it is communicated. And if the poem in which the poet's I-figure serves as an agent concretizes and conveys this sensation of emotional truth, a humanly dramatic and formally satisfying truth, then the literal truth has given birth to a thing more lasting than itself, and by which it will inevitably come to be remembered and judged.

It has always seemed to me that Plato's "The poets lie too much" should be construed as an insult of quite another kind than Plato intended. To be most genuinely damaging to the poets, the philosopher might better have said, "Our poets do not lie creatively enough; I prefer the real world untouched by their fabrications based upon it." For it is within the authentic magic of fabrication (a making-up as a making) that the I-figure moves, for as he receives his kind of reality—both an imposed and a *discovered* reality—from the poet and from language, so his being, his memorability, and his *effect* increase, and his place in his only world is more nearly assured.

The reader, on the other hand, knows that the thing he is dealing with is a *poem*, and not a news bulletin; therefore he can enjoy the luxury of submitting to it; that is, of abandoning his preconceptions about reality and entering into the poem's, for whatever there might be in it for him.

It is quite possible that I am oversimplifying, and drawing the lines too sharply. If the personality and being of the I-figure and the poet himself were *entirely* separate from each other, it would be much easier to discuss the two. But, of course, that is not—and could not be—the case. What happens is that the poet comes on a part of himself inadvertently; he surprises this part and then uses it, and, as he uses it, he more fully discovers it. For instance, suppose that one imagined himself as questioning Wordsworth about the composition of "Tintern Abbey." And suppose the poet answered, as he might well have done, "Yes, I *did* once find myself in just such a situation, and I did, as I recollect (in tranquillity!), feel very much as the poem says I did." And yet the point to note here is that the emotion could not possibly have presented itself, at the time of which it speaks, in the particular images and rhythms of the completed poem; these were factors that were added and worked in later, much after the fact, in an attempt to give the incident some kind of objectifying scheme of reference: to present it by means of a linguistic construction which could, by virtue of the fact that men may communicate verbally in several ways including the poetic, make the experience in at least some ways generally available. Put another way, Wordsworth might conclude of the devices and form of his poem, "They *might be said* to convey something like what I think I remember about that day, and how I felt about it, now that I have thought of it in this way."

Let me take a more recent example—Bernard Spencer's "Ill":

Expectant at the country gate the lantern. On the night
Its silks of light strained. Lighted upper window.
"Is it you sent for me?" The two go in
To where the woman lies ill, upstairs, out of sight.

I hear sky softly smother to earth in rain,
As I sit by the controls and the car's burning dials.
And always the main-road traffic searching, searching
    the horizons.
Then those sounds knifed by the woman's Ah! of pain.

Who dreamed this; the dark folding murderer's hands
    round the lamps?
The rain blowing growth to rot? Lives passed beneath a
    ritual
That tears men's ghosts and bodies; the few healers
With their weak charms, moving here and there among
    the lamps?

Now one cannot say with certainty whether Spencer ever *did* anything like this or not, though such is the persuasiveness of the poem that one is more likely than not to believe he did. But what is certain is that he reinvented himself in order to write the poem. He put himself in a car in the dark outside a country house, and he gave this figure of himself a way of thinking, a set of images and rhythms, and above all a way of speaking that he believed were right to body forth the scene in his particular way of being a poet. We are in the poem because he is, at a definite place and time, and we experience the invisible doctor and sick woman through his reactions. What he thinks and feels are what a reflective and imaginative mind has *found* to say about the incident between the time it happened or was invented and the time the poem was completed.

The I-figure does not live in the real world of fact but in a kind of magical abstraction, an emotion- and thought-charged personal version of it. Rather than in a place where objects and people have the taciturn and indisputable tangibility, the stolid solidity, of fact, the poetic agent inhabits a realm more rich and strange and a good deal "thicker" than reality, for it gathers to itself all the analogies and associations—either obvious or farfetched—that the poetic mind as it ranges through the time and space of its existence can bring to the subject. Constrained only by the laws imposed on him by the situation of any and all types, from the most matter-of-fact sort of reporting to the wildest phantasmagoria, he can be whatever his poem needs him to be. It is by virtue of his having his existence in just such a specialized kind of linguistic fiction that the I-figure—and in another way the poet—becomes what he is: a man subject to the permutations and combinations of words, to the vicissitudes of denotation and connotation. Both are creatures trapped by grammar, and also at the mercy of its expressive possibilities and those of all the particulars and means of the poem. The poet is also a man who has a new or insufficiently known part of himself released by these means. He is set free, for he is more inclusive than before; he is greater than he was.

A STATEMENT OF LONGING

THE SON, THE CAVE, AND
THE BURNING BUSH

"Young poet" is a term that enjoys a particular favor. Everyone who cares about poetry hopes that each young or new poet to appear on the scene may be the one to bring forth the whole magnificent potential of poetry and lay it on the page, and thus realize the promise that poetry makes in age after age but seldom succeeds in keeping. This is the promise to bring the reader to the place where the flame breaks forth from the pit and the gods speak from the burning bush, lifting human words from their mereness, out of the range of teachable amenities and into the realm of salvation, redemption and rebirth. Such is the promise of the fifty-four young American poets collected in this anthology.

For a middle-aged poet like myself this promise takes on a particularly acute anguish of hope. In fact, the potential of the poems represented here is more exciting to an older poet than it is, possibly, for anyone but the young poets themselves. The aging process almost always brings to the poet the secret conviction that he has settled for far too little, that he has paid too much attention to the "limitations" that his contemporaries have assured him he has, as well as to literary tradition and the past. He believes that either he has given unnecessary attention to these things or that he has not learned to get the most out of them. The nearer he gets to his end the more he yearns for the cave: for a wild, shaggy, all-out, all-involving way of speaking where language and he (or, now, someone: some new poet) engage each other at primitive levels, on ground where the issues are not those of literary fashion but are quite literally those of life and death. All his lifelong struggle with "craft" seems a tragic and ludicrous waste of time; and he looks on the productions of the whole history of literature—indeed, of all human communication and expression—as so much self-indulgent and irrelevant chatter in the unspeaking and accusing face of what *could* be said, if someone had the luck, the vision and the guts.

It is a sad dream; but one that gathers force. The young or new poet, like the son real or imagined, holds out the prospect of hope, of that kind of engagement with language that older poets feel they have—with the best will in the world, with much toil and conscientiousness—betrayed. Teaching the "craft of verse" for years, as many of our older and middle generation of American poets have done, only increases the irrational longing for the unwritten and perhaps unwritable poem. Anyone who cares for poetry enough to write and teach it all his life wants it to be capable of more than he has ever been able to make poetry do: more than has ever been dreamed of in the seminar's philosophy. What he wants to hear is nothing less than the poetry of the burning bush. If he lives long enough, the poet comes to believe in the rarest of possibilities that, once seen, no longer seems rare but simply a miracle—something like the cave man's identification of the red deer on the wall of the cave with the one miles away on the plain. The older poet looks for signs beyond those that have been given, and certainly beyond those that he has been able to give. He looks to the new poets.

And so, when a writer of my age picks up an anthology like this, it is with the feeling: "Maybe it is here." Most of these poets are young, and all of them are comparatively new, insofar as academic or beer-hall discussion, anthologies, publication and reputation are concerned. But it seems to me that almost all of them have the kind of vitality, linguistic and physical, that is as exciting as anything in poetry can be, save the Poetry of the Impossible: the burning bush itself.

The enormous variety of these fifty-four poets is not *just* variety. It is a kind of variety with significance: for the conformity of sensibility that has overlain and undermined poetry in the English language since Pound and Eliot is gone. The withdrawnness and the literarily connoisseurish stance—the poet waiting in the crafty lair of his sensibility poring over books for his ideas—is not much in evidence here among these young poets. Their poems are not merely reworkings of known and established forms; they are personal explorations for which, most of the time, there is no precedent. For this reason a good many of them may seem somewhat rough-edged or ragged and even on occasion naive: the smoothness of the poem in which all the chinks have been carefully filled in is notably absent. But at the stage of things where we now are in American poetry, too much smoothness is suspect, and the carpentered poem is slowly becoming synonymous with the predictable and inconsequential one. The techniques of these poets vary a good deal, as they should, but what ought to be noted is that there is a new and refreshing concentration on content as well: here, the "what" matters as much as the "how," and in some cases more. Turning the pages of this book, one muses and drops back into the kind of revery that may produce everything or nothing. Could the voice that spoke to Moses have benefitted from a course in Modern Rhetoric? And what if Dylan Thomas had gone to school in a writers' workshop in an American university to learn how to write poetry?

And yet technique matters, even so. God uses it, for a buffalo is not a leopard; as my grandmother used to say, "He is made different." God and the angels use technique, only it is better than ours, and operates on better materials. The divine technique is both consummate technique that no one has ever heard of, and beyond all considerations of technique. All roads are long, as Allen Tate says, and in the end they lead to the problem of form. The poets in this book are working on, around and through the problem of form; and it should be obvious from a look through these pages—a flipping, even—that some of them appear to have wandered into old or dead-end streets. For example, there are some attempts here at the kind of calculated boldness that one associates with the experimentalism of the 1920s. On the other hand, a few of them have tried to write rather complacent formal exercises in rhyme and regular meter that show into what a mortuary a misunderstood classicism can lead poems. And it is of course possible that the huge and ghostly figures of Eliot and Pound may hover around many of these poems in ways that the poets would be the last to suspect (and not as entirely baleful influences, either, for one must not forget the very real value of their examples). But the important thing to note is that the writers in this anthology are attempting in a new way to speak with as much real boldness as they can summon of passion and involvement, rather than in the distant and learnedly disdainful tone of Eliot or with the manic scholarliness of Pound.

Most of these poets do not seem to be as informed or well-read as some of the best poets who immediately preceded them. Not one of them has the sheer amount of information that Randall Jarrell had when he began writing, nor the grasp of European history that Robert Lowell had, nor the knowledge of prosody with which Karl Shapiro or John Berryman began, nor Auden's spectacular ability to generalize. Auden and Jarrell, like the fox of the Russian fable, know many things; but each of these poets, like the hedgehog of the same fable, feel that he knows one *big* thing: what it is to *be*, in a particular skin and at a particular time and place; and what it is like to respond with directness and passion, beyond or to the side of established literary precedent. Sometimes this happens with an earthiness and vulgarity that probably would have caused Mr. Eliot to shudder. But the too-close world of sweat and sperm and yelling and drunkenness, the precarious realm of betrayal and that of true and deep encounters between human beings is always with us, is always possible, with or without archetypal significations and symbolical precedents, and that is where most of these poets are living and writing.

I have no wish to talk about "schools" or movements, real or fancied. It is enough for me that this anthology gives a various and exciting voice to a poetic generation that insists on its full right to its human responses, as well as on its right to make mistakes, and above all on its right to fly in the face of the graduate-school's well-documented notion of what is "proper" and of what is commonly designated "literature." These poems seem to me to be evidence that imposed styles are not, finally, the shapers of the sensibilities of men. Such styles may appear to be so for a while, and sometimes for a long while. But in the end the animal responsiveness of individuals breaks through. This is what saves poetry from itself and from its practitioners and theorists; this is what creates change and makes of poetry a fluid and volatile condition where anything can happen.

And if the Voice from the Bush is not here (and it may be, subject only to the discovery of Time) it is not the fault of these poets. Such clearness and passion as theirs has not been heard in a long time, in our land and in our language. If the Lost Son with the Angel's tongue does not dwell in these pages, let us regret it doubly, for some of these lines hint how he might speak. These young American poets are with and *in* human experience as poets have not been for a very long time.

TWO TALKS IN WASHINGTON

1 METAPHOR AS PURE ADVENTURE

The longer I continue to write, the more it seems to me that the most exciting thing about poetry is its sense of imminent and practical discovery. With this in mind, and also in view of the fact that I am the one giving the lecture this evening, it might be interesting to look for a little while at the kinds of discoveries that poetry, with luck, makes possible and at what happens when the poet asks parts of creation to get together, not with the consent of the Almighty, but simply because he asks them to.

Let me begin with a passage from a favorite novel of mine, *The Time of Man*, by Elizabeth Madox Roberts. This is the first paragraph of the book.

> Ellen wrote her name in the air with her finger, *Ellen Chesser*, leaning forward and writing on the horizontal plane. Beside her in the wagon her mother huddled under an old shawl to keep herself from the damp, complaining, "We ought to be a-goen on."

This is a primitive—but to me very moving—way of self-definition and could stand for the kind of thing every poet is attempting to do: write his name on the air. But in the case of poets the important thing to notice is that self-definition is not a matter of formulaic or any other permanent kind of restrictive attitude but is rather a thing of the moment: as though, if one were to understand the self of the moment, one might thereby understand something of the essential self. One may never apprehend the whole of the self, as if the self might be uncovered in its entirety, bit by bit, as one strips the trivia away. The relation of poetry—and of metaphor—to the self is not like this at all. It is a matter of moments, and of the conjunctions that may be born of the moment, and illuminate the moment, and then come to stand for one of the ways in which the moment may strike to the heart of time itself. As Blake said, "Eternity is in love with the productions of time."

The deliberate conjunction of disparate items which we call metaphor is not so much a way of understanding the world but a perpetually exciting way of recreating it from its own parts, as though God—who admittedly did it right the first time—had by no means exhausted the possibilities. It is a way of causing the items of the real world to act upon each other, to recombine, to suffer and learn from the mysterious value systems, or value-making systems, of the individual, both in his socially conditioned and in his inmost, wild, and untutored mind. It is a way of putting the world together according to rules which one never fully understands, but which are as powerfully compelling as anything in the whole human makeup. Making metaphors is like operating according to dictates—and even here I am reasoning by "likes" as one will do—which are imperatives, but which are not fully comprehended, but mainly felt; imperatives which simply *present* themselves, not in the form of codified *dicta*, but as modes of action in *that* particular context: "Put *this* word with that one rather than the other one. It is *these* two things that you want to compare, not those two."

I conceive of poetry not so much as a matter of serene and disinterested choice but of action, and the very *heat* of choice. I think of the poem as a kind of action in which, if the poet can participate *enough*, other people cannot help participating as well. I am against all marmoreal, closed, to-be-contemplated kinds of poems and conceive of the poem as a minute part of the Heraclitean flux, and of the object of the poem as not to slow or fix or limit the flux at all but to try as it can to preserve and implement the "fluxness," the flow, and show this moving through the poem, coming in at the beginning and going back out, after the end, into the larger, nonverbal universe whence it came. I am everywhere aware of relation, connection, with one object shedding a light—a more or less strong, a more or less interesting light—on another. It is at least fairly interesting to say, "Stages—ah, stages and . . . and *mountains!*" Or better still, plateaus! There is a certain similarity of form: people in the Bible are always making speeches from mountains; there are lots of stage-precedents and mountain-precedents that one can, if one is an Eliotic traditionalist . . . But no, that is not really very interesting, after all. When carried away in this kind of vein, it is best to heed the warning implicit in the great story of the Argentinian writer Jorge Luis Borges, "The Handwriting of God." Borges asks you to note that each single thing implies the whole universe. If you think of the jaguar, you also imply the herds of deer on which the jaguar fed, the grass that nourished those herds, the rain that fell on the grass, and finally the whole eternal process that caused the jaguar, the single jaguar, to be. The poetic method of connecting things, however, cannot really be this broad. To be satisfactory to the poet, metaphor must connect items according to a more rigorous and profoundly personal way than mere arbitrary juxtaposition. The question is, in *what* way?

I have pondered this question a good while because it interests me, and because I thought that if perhaps I clarified the issue somewhat in my own mind, I could move with less obvious waste. One evening, while pondering "weak and weary" over many a volume of theoretical lore, I came on the following statement by the modern French poet, Pierre Reverdy:

> Insofar as the juxtaposition of entities be separated by the greater distance, and yet be just, the metaphor will be thereby stronger.

Now, that struck me as being something like what I feel about the metaphorical relationship—something *very* like. If we could figure out, and *apply*, one word in this just-sounding aphorism, we would be a lot nearer knowing how the poetic metaphor lives. The word is "juste"—just, or apt. It is obvious that it is not awfully hard to tell when the two terms of a metaphor, the two things that are being compared or asked to live together, are far apart, as the world or the ordinary man judges. But it is not always easy to tell when the comparision between them is "juste." This is where we get back to imponderables and individual re-actions, for what may be just to me may very well be unjust, or even absurd, to you. I am willing, however, to leave it at that, because the individual sense of justness—or poetic justice—is in any given case the poetic sense it-self, or at least so far as comparison or metaphor is con-cerned. I should state here, more or less parenthetically, that I am not here concerned with textbook definitions of met-aphor, with metaphor as distinguished from simile, or anything of that kind. I take metaphor in the broad sense, as denoting any kind of comparison as a basis for the kind of illumination we call poetic. It would require a mind like Paul Valéry's or Wallace Stevens' to follow such questions at these into territories where they would begin to yield the results they deserve to yield, and I must stress what you already know: that I am not a philosopher, or even a philosophical poet. My purpose here is simply to call attention to the proclivity—nay, the compulsion—of the human mind to make comparisons, partly as a way to real or fancied knowledge or control of the subjects involved—and thus as a kind of primitive magic and personal science—but also for the sheer thrill of ingenuity, the puzzlemaking, resolving, and aesthetic excitement of the activity itself. When sportswriter Jim Mur-ray of the *Los Angeles Times* tells me, for example, that quarterback John Brodie of the San Francisco Forty-Niners is "slower than fourth-class mail," I am delighted beyond measure, not because I am gloating over Mr. Brodie's heaviness of foot but because the mind that made the comparison delights me with its energy, ingenuity, and quickness. When a movie critic says—or said, years ago—of Shirley Temple's first husband, the mercifully forgotten John Agar, that "he acts as though the idea of acting was not his in the first place," I am equally delighted and in an entirely different way, dependent not so much on watching John Brodie run on Sunday-afternoon TV as on watching old movies even later in the evening, such as Mr. Agar's opus *Ride a Crooked Mile*. As I say, I take pleasure from the aptness of these examples because I have seen the principals act out, each in his way, the metaphors. But they would be good metaphors even without John Brodie and John Agar because there will always be slow athletes and handsome, inept actors. Yea, and until the end of time!

The masters of metaphor are not, however, sportswriters and movie reviewers, but poets. The greatest, the most enduring, metaphors have been made by them. And it is fascinating, in our Age of Investigation, to see how various poets put the world together in their particular and idiosyncratic ways. There are many learned treatises on the fashions in which various poets do this, and one can go to the files of the universities in Syracuse and Buffalo and of Washington University in St. Louis—and to the files of the Library of Congress—and pore over the draft sheets and worksheets of poets to see how they have changed, patched and shaded, discarded, found, have searched thesauruses and dictionaries, have compared and contrasted, have called into play everything, literally, in the world, to help them write their poems. Sometimes you can't make much of these sheets, the poet's working habits being too private. But sometimes you can tell a good deal, though never *quite* enough. Dylan Thomas will have, say, a selection of words, one of which he may end up using in a certain place in a line, or none of which he may use. And it is fun—and instructive—to arrive at various ways of agreeing with the poet (for who would disagree with Dylan Thomas where his own work is concerned?) as to why he chose this word and discarded the others. And yet the list of words *itself* is, with Thomas, the most mysterious and provocative list ever seen and is likely to be taken by the unwary for a Thomas poem in its own right. If we could tell why Thomas selected *those* words out of which to choose (or not to choose), the poetic process, at least in the case of Thomas, would be a great deal clearer to us than it is now. But how the list came to Thomas' mind in the first place is something we shall never know; it is part of the poetic mystery, and I for one am glad that it is.

Despite the great area of the Unknowable in which poems are born and live, there are a few very broad generalizations we can make about kinds of metaphor. There is surely a generic difference, for example, between the *merely* ingenious kind of conjunction and the kind that has both the strangeness and the inevitability of poetry. When Marshall McLuhan says that the electric light bulb is "pure information," we can see what he means, but it is the sort of formulation in which the straining to be original is much more evident than the originality. Of course it is possible to look at the light bulb from the standpoint of its being "pure information," but that is not, at least to my view, particularly enlightening. The comparison of light bulb and information has the obviousness-with-a-twist that we think of, in every age, as the mark of the minor talent. When Robert Duncan says something to the effect that "the sky is not sure it is not an elephant," we feel the same sense of strain and would-be about the figure. But when D. H. Lawrence refers to a fish as a "gray, monotonous soul in the water," quite another thing happens. At first one is troubled by Lawrence's calling the fish a "soul," but then he remembers that this poet's way of looking at existence is essentially that of a personal animism. And fish *do* look gray under water. But it is the "monotonous" that is the truly poetic word. There is that wavering of the fish through the water, like a ghost and like a soul that seems almost on the point of disap-

pearing but will not go, and perhaps *cannot* go, moving with
perfect silence in his heavy, half-transparent purgatory. The
mind of the reader dilates around the image of the fish
when it is presented in this way; all kinds of imaginatively
profitable and creative connections come in. As in the case
of all good poetic figures, there are the connections that
we all make in more or less the same ways and those that
are utterly private and personal. But again, what made Law-
rence see the pike as a "gray, monotonous soul in the water"
may be guessed at, after the fact, but never really known.

The ways in which the mind associates, and the particular
materia mater out of which the associations come—the *materia
mater* that is available to the mind in toto, and the mysterious
way in which bits and pieces of this come up at a certain
time, as though there were an element of fate involved—
we know almost nothing of, and *can* know but very little.
If I were going to write about a fish, for instance, what
happens in my brain? Do all the fish I have ever seen in
my life swim to the surface for possible use? No; at best,
only a few of them come. Why those? I can't say, beyond
supposing that these must be the ones that impressed me
the most, for one reason or another. But impressed me in
what way? I simply must accept them as the most fishy
fish, the most archetypal fish I have in my mind, the Platonic
fish that will have to stand for all the rest.

That, however, is only the beginning. In my own case,
to cite the example closest to hand, the only poem I have
ever devoted to a fish, a long one called "The Shark's Parlor,"
is not about anything I have ever done or any actual fish
I ever saw. A shark has been made out of the few ham-
merheads I have ever seen in the water, those I have seen
hanging up at docks, and one I found dead on a beach.
It is not quite that these sharks combined into one in my
mind but that the dead one on the shore drew into him-
self, as my strongest mental hammerhead, all the others, so
that the others became him and contributed to him in my
mind, where I then attempted to place him in another kind

of sea, in a poem, and cause him to live and act there. But my apprehension of my shark was conditioned, as it must inevitably be, by what experiences, including pictures in books and dreams, I have had in other places and other times—and perhaps other lives—with sharks. The poem was also influenced, in what ways it is hard for me to tell, by a movie called *The Shark Fighters*, which starred, if I remember correctly, Victor Mature. All of these things came together into the passionate and mysterious aura of association that this kind of fish had for *me*. And from these mixed sources I made a poem about an imaginary incident.

The pure adventurousness of making metaphors and poems is a condition that must be felt to be believed. I remember how tremendously excited I was when I first formulated to myself the proposition that the poet is not to be limited by the literal truth: that he is not trying to *tell* the truth: he is trying to *make* it. Therefore he is absolutely free, in the sense of the definition of creativity as the capacity to act according to laws of one's own devising. When one grasps this, the feeling of liberation and the attendant devotion to one's own vision are so exciting that the dedication of a life to following these things wherever they may lead seems a small enough endeavor, the least that one can do. For what the poet is trying to accomplish is to discover relationships that give life: mental, physical, and imaginative life, the fullest and most electric sense of being.

One begins with the sensible world, which in its entirety is a gift, and a gift also in each of its parts. As far as I am concerned, that is as good a definition as can be given of a poet: that he is one who feels the world as a gift. But there is a second gift that you give yourself, based on the world's great gift. I often wonder how Adam felt—or the earliest man felt—when he closed his eyes and saw that the world was still there, inside his head. That is the most miraculous thing in the whole of existence to me: those pictures of the world inside one's head; pictures made of the real world, but pictures that one *owns*, that one infuses with one's own personality. They are fragments of the world that live, not with the world's life, but with ours.

But I am not here, so my announced subject tells me, to talk about the image, as much as I would like to, but to talk about comparisons of one thing to another and about the part that language plays in the kinds of comparisons that we call poetic metaphors. But almost all metaphors begin with pictures in the head. Now these pictures, these entities, are, first of all, possessions of ours. We have paid nothing for them, but we *have* them, in the magic CinemaScope of the mind; we have them because they are there, and no one can banish them except ourselves—and even that is doubtful, for when we attempt to banish them, we may very well simply be making them obsessive.

If we are poets—that is, *conscious* poets—we are interested in three things concerning these fragments of the world as they have come to us. First, we wish to find threads of continuity running through them, threads of consequence and meaning which may work out into a narrative or dramatic action or at least into a distinct relationship that the items have obtained, not from their position and interrelationship in the "real" world, but purely from us. The second thing we look for (or perhaps I should say *I* look for) is a way to recombine these elements so that they undergo a fruitful interchange of qualities, a transference of energies, an informing of each other. The greatest poets have the greatest power to do this, as when Gerard Manley Hopkins compares the longest flame of a bonfire to a whip, or speaks of thunder rolling its *floors* of sound. Without Hopkins there would never have been any particularly illuminating connection between thunder and floors, but *with* Hopkins there is a startling connection: one sees and hears the justness of the comparison immediately, though each apprehends it in his own way, depending upon what thunders (and floors) he has known. The third thing the poet tries to do is to introduce his vital, necessary, and incomparable element, language, into this thread-discovering and -connecting process that he is engaged in. And here the difficulties are very great and the excitement and sense of adventure correspondingly intense. For when the poet is, as W. S. Graham beautifully says, "trusted on the language," he is both submitting to and consciously working with a medium he prefers, much as the partners in lovemaking are both submitting to and working with each other. The poet is committing himself to making his discoveries in *this* way: the way of words in a certain order, and with a certain informing spirit which he hopes will be his; for if it is not his, it is nothing.

Now when things are compared linguistically, they are never quite what they were in isolation from each other or in the non-verbal context of the world. As we all know, words are signs for things, but they have at least two ranges of signification. When the poet says "tree," for example, we all presumably see a tree, somewhere in the head. But the second range of signification is not universal but personal and private: we don't all see the same tree. In fact, *none* of us sees the same tree. This is one thing about poetic imagery that has bothered some people, for they wish to submit, or reduce, the poetic act to a condition based upon which "scientific" or universal judgments may be made about it and about the individual poems that it produces. It has bothered some people, but I don't believe it has ever bothered any poet; or at any rate any real poet. For, as John Keats says, "What shocks the virtuous philosopher, delights the chameleon poet." Poets think it a kind of double good fortune that they may ask each of their readers, not to see the poet's tree, but to supply one from his own life, and to bring it —as a gift—into the poem.

The making of poetic metaphors is an intrinsic process: a continual process of transfiguring reality. For example, having encountered Hopkins' thunder as the rolling of "great floors of sound," I am neither in the presence exclusively of either thunder, or floors, or sounds, nor yet of rolling, as isolated entities or actions. I cease to experience the thunder alone (either real thunder or mental thunder), or the floors alone, but I enter into a magical secondary state, an enriched reality made possible by the conjunction of these items, by the comparison where thunder, floors, sounds, and rolling are, so to speak, together in a new kinship made possible by a special use of language, but having, also, a sort of kinship in the mind which seems to me to be extra-linguistic as well, having to do only with the things themselves. When I have apprehended this new relationship, have brought my own thunders and my own floors to it, my mind then roams round and about this new relationship in a different world from one I can open my eyes and see, or unstuff my ears and hear, and all this is qualified and amplified by the pleasure I take in the newness and aptness of Hopkins' figure of speech and the feeling of extension that it provokes in me. It is another emotional dimension that I have been given—a present—and my main attitude toward it is simple gratitude.

For these reasons, and many others, the ways of making comparisons, metaphors, figures of speech, and so on, are subject to none but the very broadest of rules, and even these must be liberally interpreted. If we could codify the metaphor-making process, we would all be able to write like Hopkins—or indeed anybody else we wanted to. It is because of the utter impossibility of codifying and making generally available an authentically poetic way of comparing, of making genuinely original metaphors, that poetry is and will always be entirely different from science. Again, the aura of association about specific words differs greatly from person to person. The particular kind of getting-together-of-things that I characterize as poetic results in a variety of insight that is, though not scientific, nonetheless of very great value to those equipped to receive it. I don't want to turn this evening into a "Defence of Poesie," for poetry can defend itself quite well enough, but I *would* like to lay down the few generalizations about metaphor that I have been able to glean from the years.

First, the terms of a metaphor are almost always concrete and *one* of them *is* always concrete; that is, the terms are parts of the given world. A correspondence is established between already created things.

Second, this correspondence carries an emotional charge, or rather two of them: a general one which anyone might be expected to respond to, and another one to which any individual, in his particular life situation, is free to respond out of those specific conditions which have resulted in his being who he is.

Third, the true metaphor orients the mind toward freedom and novelty; it encourages the mind to be daring. And at the same time the metaphor furnishes the mind with at least the illusion of a new kind of relational necessity, as well as giving it the joy—the pure joy—of employing faculties that are not used in conceptual language.

If I may go a little further into abstraction, I would also say that metaphor permits one to experience at the same time the perpetual and the instantaneous, the paired objects both in the world they came from and in their linguistic relationship in the poem.

But it is not really my purpose to generalize, in the manner of the seminar room, about a subject as mysterious as metaphor. I had rather simply talk about the very great delight in making metaphorical relations at any level at all. And delight it *is*. That is why poets don't want to go to Heaven: they are already there the day they are born as earthly creatures. I remember with affection the words of the all-but-forgotten American painter Charles Burchfield, who was asked, a few months before he died, how he felt about "eternal life." He said, "I don't know anything about it. But I hope there is painting there."

As for poets, I don't believe it is possible for men to conceive—or for God to conceive—of a better universe for poets and poetry than the one we have. But the natural order of things *is* the natural order. A river is not a stone, and a tree is not a star; nor is a woman a tigress (that is, not *literally*). But poets believe, with a high secret glee, that precisely because God made these things as they are (the star, the tree, the woman), because He made them so much themselves that they can be nothing *but* themselves, someone else—someone like a poet, say—can come along and compare a star to a woman, or to a tree, and accomplish something valuable by it. Poets believe that the things of this world are capable of making connections between each other that not God but men see, and they say so. Stars, stones, and trees have no emotional charge in themselves, but a very powerful one for men. To Matthew Arnold, to the ancient Greek tragedians, and to many other human beings the sound of the sea on pebbles brings "the eternal note of sadness in." And it is in the language of metaphor charged with specific emotions that the poet makes his statement and creates, out of the world as it is, the world that he must, because he is what he is, bring to birth. Much has been written of the agonies of creation, but to at least one poet it seems the most delightful, exciting, and natural act in the world, a kind of perpetual and pure adventure.

For the world without the play of the mind over it is a dull place indeed. After all, rocks are only inert matter, trees are only stolid wood that sways a little in the air according to the natural law of the wind. Stars are only burning chemicals, and a woman is only a collocation of animal cells formed into the female humanity-reproducing beast. It is the mind itself, in its quick and intimate and original presence, that turns the universe into a magical arena, or, as Keats called it, "a vale of soul-making." If I had only one point to make this evening, it would be in favor of imaginative participation in the cosmos. As D. H. Lawrence says in *Apocalypse*, "We have lost the cosmos." What I take this to mean is that Lawrence believes we no longer have any vital relationship to the universe, and he is very likely right. He thinks, also, that we can only possess the cosmos by an act of worship. This seems to me to be perfectly true. And if we believe, with Kafka, that "all writing is a form of prayer," then we would have to agree that the poets have been praying the longest, although perhaps not the loudest. The poet's form of worship is both descriptive and relational; he imbues the cosmos so strongly with his own emotions that he believes that, in return, the cosmos allows him to recombine its elements in his own way, largely for the sheer delight of it—for the adventure.

As I said earlier, it is lovely to engage in the relational adventure at any level, from the serviceman's or fraternity boy's search—a very real one—to describe sexual intercourse (there *have* been some good tries), or from the whole male sex's eternal quest to find a truly adequate name for the female sex organ, at which we have failed abjectly, through the rather ordinary quips in *Reader's Digest* ("He had a face like an unmade bed"), up through the superhumanly brilliant epic similes and metaphors of Homer and Virgil and Lucretius and Dante and Milton. If I had time, I'd like to make for you a little anthology of my favorite metaphors and tell you just what I like about them (though of course I don't know *completely*, in any given case, why I like what I like). I can't do that, of course, but neither can I resist giving you a few of the best. And my fondest hope is that you will begin collecting comparisons, as I have done all my life, and I hope also that you will never accept any but the best ones: the ones that have it, as the hippies say, for *you*. These are some that have it—*it*—for me.

When William Strode, who lived just after Shakespeare, says

> Nor snow when falling from the sky
> Hovers in its virginity

he has made a connection between a fact of nature and humanity that counts.

When Milton says of the angel Raphael that he

> Comes this way moving; seems another morn
> Risen on mid-noon

you have seen, as Adam did, an angel come to you. How could an angel come in any other way, at noon?

When Edgar Allan Poe—yes, even Edgar Allan Poe—refers to the sea as

That wilderness of glass

something has truly changed in your perception and experience of the sea—and also in your perception and experience of glass, and of wildernesses.

When Tennyson speaks of the sea into which the sea-buried corpse is flung, and says that the shotted body

Drops in its vast and wandering grave

you know something else again, about the sea, about the poor human body, and about death.

And when the blues singer, Scrapper Blackwell, invites someone to

Put your arms around me like a circle round the sun

you never want to love in any other way.

Well, these are just a few instances of individual aptness of perception having to do with parts of the world in a new relation made possible by seeing and saying them in a particular way.

Let me reiterate: find your own metaphors. Or better still, *make* your own. Just to get you started, let me give you a problem to work on. See if you can find the combination of things and words, the objective and unobjective correlatives, to get this scene said. (I expect to get some mail on this, I conjure you!)

This is a kind of scene out of early adolescence: mine. I was walking along a beach in south Georgia, and for some reason or other I had half a loaf of stale bread in my hand. It was low tide. The sea was flat and low, a "wilderness of glass," in fact. There was a sandbar about a hundred yards from where I was, and I walked out through the water toward it, through schools of minnows. Now, I don't know how all this grabs you, but it's had hold of *me* for years, especially lately, for it is so obviously a Dickey kind of subject: a large scene from nature, forms of alien life, fish, sun, silence, and—a loaf of bread. Can you do anything with that? It's a Dickey poem, but Dickey can't seem to write it.

Anyway, I got out to the sandbar and tore off a piece of bread and gave it to a sea gull. He rose and hovered and came back, and for a while I kept throwing pieces of bread into the air, and he'd sweep by and catch them. Then he reproduced himself in mid-air—ah! maybe we could use *that!*—what I mean is that there were two of him, then five, then dozens, then hundreds. One of him hit me in the back of the head like a sledgehammer—no; we need a better comparison here: there *must* be one!—and I suddenly realized that if I didn't do something to protect myself I'd be likely to lose an eye or two. At least I ought to give up the rest of the bread. But I didn't. I stood there on the sandbar covered with wings and beaks, and kept pitching up the bread in smaller and smaller pieces until it was all gone, and the birds reluctantly, slowly dispersed, and I was there alone, shook up and happy, with a moderately bloody head.

Now, I've never been able to get any kind of metaphorical meaning out of this incident, or indeed any kind of meaning that seemed to have poetic possibilities. But it strikes me now that it could be a metaphor for metaphor itself: the gulls may—*may*—be likened to fragments of the world which come at the poet from all sides—the world's beautiful and dangerous gifts—sometimes threatening him, not in themselves caring for him, but bearing their presences in on him just the same. The poet is the man with the bread—that is, with the means of attracting them to himself, the bread being the imagination that calls them and feeds them. Again, maybe calling the gulls was my own way of writing on the air: of writing my name on the air, with bread, blood, and wings.

And yet I am not satisfied with that, quite. It is a little too pat, too serviceable, too one-dimensional. As I say, I'm not satisfied with it; it is merely the best I have been able to do. And I expect that things will remain so, in regard to this particular unwritten poem. That is, until I hear from you.

2 SPINNING THE CRYSTAL BALL

Somehow or other, poets always find themselves at bay: before critics, before other poets, before well-meaning ladies at cocktail parties, before talk-show MCs and publishers and wives and friends and novelists. In fact, poets *like* to be at bay: it is sort of their natural habitat. They are always at the edge, and what they do there, besides writing poems, is express their opinions. These present remarks are offered not so much from the vantage of any particular height, but merely from an involvement in the situation from which the future must inevitably come, whether it comes from my part of, or part in, the situation or not. It is a kind of speech which will try to combine a certain more or less hopefully shrewd guesswork and blindly emotional prejudice; that is, it will be partly about what I think might happen in American poetry and what I hope *will* happen. And if the speech turns out to be clairvoyant, I will be more surprised than any of you.

Well, first of all, how does one usually predict? From empirical evidence, mainly. One tries to say what will be from an examination of what has been, as it operates on what is now, and as these two examinable bodies of evidence seem to indicate a continuation of one through the other: a kind of vector that points in a certain direction. But again, before I plunge into the weird world of assessments and predictions, let me stress once more the purely personal nature of these remarks; if certain affinities and allegiances color what I say, I would like to believe that these may be taken simply as evidence of involvement, of caring.

To proceed from the available evidence, rather than from preference, we can look first at the "confessional" school, or what I should be tempted to call "the poetry of personal complaint." The most prominent figure of this group is Robert Lowell, but his work is already so well known in this and other regards that it would be better, here, to look at some of its results: at how his influence operates in the work of those who are seeking to continue it and extend it. When one reads W. D. Snodgrass, Anne Sexton, and, most particularly, Sylvia Plath, one thing strikes one before anything else does. The impulse behind the poetry appears to be—and no doubt is—essentially therapeutic: one variation or another of the famous statement of D. H. Lawrence's, "One sheds one's sicknesses in books." The material is pretty much the same as that which furnishes the conversation of the psychoanalytical encounter and the desperate phone call to the best friend whom the caller simply will not—cannot —let go until he or she has poured out the whole awful truth, with all the physical details of humiliation, and the rest. The notion here, no new one to either analyst or bartender, or in fact to anyone else, is that if one can get it out, can share it, that is, *describe* it, one can alleviate the intolerable pain of the condition one describes. An analogy that occurs to me in this connection is, oddly enough, the recent book by William Manchester on the assassination of President Kennedy. The fascination of the book is that it functions as a kind of rite of exorcism. People feel that if the terrible event is known, fully known, down to the least detail of who stood where, what this one wore, and what the other one thought, that day in Dallas will then deliver its secret, the secret that everyone believes it has, *must* have. So with these poets. *My* complaint against the poets of personal complaint is not that they are confessional, in the

sense of being engaged in a true encounter with the hor-
rible depths that everyone has, with the compulsive hatreds
that tear us apart, but that they are not confessional enough.
They are slickly confessional; they are glib. They do not
really offer the "real life"—as opposed to "literary life"—
they purport to do; they are astonishingly literary—and
here I mean literary in the bad sense—despite their insist-
ence on "ordinary life." Here are a few excerpts from a
poem by Sylvia Plath, called "Fever 103."

> Pure? What does it mean?
> The tongues of hell
>
> Are dull, dull as the triple
> Tongues of dull, fat Cerberus
> Who wheezes at the gate.
>
> .   .   .
>
> the low smokes roll
> From me like Isadora's scarves . . .

—Isadora Duncan, and her bizarre death—

> Greasing the bodies of adulterers
> Like Hiroshima ash . . .

—one must get that in, some way—

> The sheets grow heavy as a lecher's kiss.

And so on. The main feeling that one has—or at least that
I have—is of an attempt to be clever; and if there is one
thing that I find intolerable in either literature or in the
world, it is slick, knowing patter about suffering and guilt,
particularly about one's own.

This is a limited and solipsistic approach to poetry, luxuriat-
ing in and hiding behind the supposition on the reader's part
that the poet has actually suffered what the poem describes.
One can surely sympathize with that part of it, as one would
sympathize with the person whether a poet or not. It is the

way in which the suffering is presented which so falsifies it, and which the reader will not easily forgive. The more he believes the personal situation, the less he believes the poem. I think, though, that the confessional poem, as a kind of poem, is near the end of its tenure. Who could outdo Robert Lowell at this? One must, in the end, be more than a follower, if one is a true poet.

The confessional poets believe in Life, in *their* life, rather than in Art. Out on the West Coast, at that bastion of American neoclassicism, Stanford University, they believe in Art; they believe in "the mind" and in its capacity to make sense of experience and to embody that sense in verse which proceeds by means of the rational faculties. They are poets of classical severity and a surprising degree of wit. They are not chaotic, nor arbitrary, and if they despair, they despair in extremely educated ways. This is part of a sequence by J. V. Cunningham:

> It was in Vegas. Celibate and able
> I left the silver dollars on the table
> And tried the show. The black-out, baggy pants,
> Of course, and then this answer to romance:
> Her ass twitching as if it had the fits,
> Her gold crotch grinding, her athletic tits,
> One clock, the other counter clockwise twirling.
> It was enough to stop a man from girling.

One like this! The true horror of the educated, sensitive man is to confront something like the gold crotch of Las Vegas: it is exactly the kind of encounter that the neoclassic wit needs, that calls forth his best powers, including his powers of versification and rhyme. Verse is here a medium of control rather than of confession, but it is no less an exorcism than the poems of Lowell. The exorcism is in the control, as McLuhan might say, but I don't think has yet said. We might make a point or two here about the inter-action of literary technique and personality, which has always interested me very much. It seems to me that literary techniques not only express but alter the personality fully as much as the personality determines the techniques. "As he *is*, so he writes," as Coleridge said. To write as Cunningham does requires a special use of the intelligence, a great deal of schooling, a belief in the poem as a conserver rather than as a releaser of energies and insights, and it often requires also a classical education. For example, this is a translation by Cunningham of a poem by the Latin poet Janus Vitalis Panormitanus, whom I'd never heard of before, much less tried to pronounce. It is called "Rome." Think of this, ye tourists!

> You that a stranger in mid-Rome seek Rome
> And can find nothing in mid-Rome of Rome,
> Behold this mass of walls, these abrupt rocks,
> Where the vast theatre lies overwhelmed.
> Here, here is Rome! Look how the very corpse
> Of greatness still imperiously breathes threats!
> The world she conquered, strove herself to conquer,
> Conquered that nothing be unconquered by her.
> Now conqueror Rome's interred in conquered Rome,
> And the same Rome conquered and conqueror.
> Still Tiber stays, witness of Roman fame
> Still Tiber flows on swift waves to the sea.
> Learn hence what Fortune can: the unmoved falls,
> And the ever-moving will remain forever.

That is cool, beautiful, and final, and the shifts and sleights of meaning that occur from one use to the other of the verbs and nouns having to do with conquest are quite beyond the conception of any but an extremely subtle and skillful intelligence (and I would hazard a guess that they are also beyond the powers of the original Latin poet as well). Poems of this sort come out of an essentially humanistic attitude, an attitude which admits to the limitedness and perhaps vanity of human knowledge. And yet, when we read the other, mostly younger, practitioners of this approach to the poem, how dry and pedantic they seem! There are not many Cunninghams among them. Many seem to be without any kind of significant subject matter, though they know the conventions of verse perhaps better than they are known in most other schools. But as a kind of practice having possibilities of influencing the future, this approach is not a good bet. It requires more reading, more delicacy of nuance, more control, than most other kinds. Furthermore, it also appears that more and more gifts are expended to bring forth less and less obviously valuable results. It seems to me that the neoclassicists are a minority group and will remain so. It may be that people are tired of too much conscious manipulation in poems; skill, particularly of the obviously mannered sort, becomes boring, so that even a magnificent poet like Gerard Manley Hopkins palls a bit, because his poems are so obviously *poems*, literature. Most of the better young poets on both sides of the Atlantic tend to reject this kind of mannerism—including what many of them regard as the mannerism of rhyme—as not only unnecessary but in a certain sense misleading, even immoral. For example, one of the very best of the new poets, the Canadian David Wevill, who now lives and writes in England, had this to say, in answer to some questions asked him on the BBC Third Programme concerning the traditional formal disciplines of English poetry:

I respect them, but I don't feel drawn to employ them. I think because by experience I've learnt that they don't really suit my needs and that I'd much rather pay greater attention to individual words and phrases and cadences, and that the moment I strait-jacket myself with a strict form or metre I'm not free to say what I want to say. This doesn't mean that one writes in a completely undisciplined way, but you've then got to impose your own set of rules and that's a very personal thing.

Now this is an important point, this "very personal thing," this way of substituting one's own cadences for more predictable or traditional ones, and insisting on them to the extent of excluding received modes of writing. Wevill is a real poet, and his individuality as a writer is evident and at the same time is available only to himself. I suspect that this is as it should be. The American writers who want to break with tradition, however—as one might have predicted —want to lay down manifestoes of one kind or another and form "groups," publish their own magazines, and go through the whole familiar "bit" of organizing things. This is the case with the group of poets led by Charles Olson and including writers like Robert Creeley, Edward Dorn, and, to some extent, Denise Levertov. Olson's theories are more interesting than his verse or most of that of his followers. One is never sure that one understands it! He has all kinds of notions about the relationship of "the line" to breathing and other bodily processes, and he uses a curious and perhaps private vocabulary to talk about them. Here is an example, as well known as any other:

A poem is energy transferred from where the poet got it (he will have some several causations), by way of the poem itself to, all the way over to, the reader.

Well, at this point, the reader agrees: Okay, okay, but so what? Olson then says:

Then the poem itself must, at all points, be a high energy-construct and, at all points, an energy-discharge.

This seems to me to display a certain degree of naivete. When Olson uses a term like "energy-construct," he supposes himself to be using a scientific vocabulary, but what he is in fact using is a layman's idea of scientific lingo, or jargon. Who would not want to believe, for example, that poetry is "energy" in this sense, or indeed in any other? But Olson's is a specialized and prejudicial use of the term, and it is, semantically, absolutely meaningless. What this kind of usage represents is the effort—perhaps inadvertent, but symptomatic nonetheless—of a basically unscientific mind to "dignify" or at least make acceptable to his science-cowed followers and readers a thing (poetry) which is not scientific at all, that is, not subject to empirical "proof," but which is intimate and personal, subjective. If it be argued that subjectivity itself is subject to scientific investigation, one would then have to come up with the means of measuring or assessing the kind of "energy"—some sort of psychic or imaginative energy, I suppose—which Olson posits, and it is not difficult to see the absurdity of this.

But the test of all theories of poetry is the kind of poetry they produce, and this is where Olson and his followers seem to me to fail all but abjectly. Their work has absolutely no personal rhythm to it; it all comes out of the tiresome and predictable prosiness of William Carlos Williams. It is the sort of thing—as Randall Jarrell once remarked—that you use to illustrate to a class the fact that the sports page of the daily paper can be rendered into accentual-syllabic verse by cutting it into "lines."

The other "movement" around is the one headed up by Robert Bly, out of Madison, Minnesota. As professional soldiers say of the particular war they're fighting in at the time, "It ain't much, but it's the only one we got." Bly believes that the salvation of English poetry is to be found in non-English poetry, particularly in Spanish and French and German, understood as badly as possible. One does translations, taking as many liberties as one wants to take with the original, it being understood that this enables one somehow to approach the "spirit" of the poet one is translating. If I had time I would talk some about surrealism, for the French and Spanish surrealist poets are very much the bellwethers of the Bly faction. But it might be better to quote a couple of things to show you the end results. This is Bly's "Approaching Winter."

I

September. Clouds. The first day for wearing jackets.
The corn is wandering in dark corridors,
Near the well and the whisper of tombs.

II

I sit alone surrounded by dry corn,
Near the second growth of the pigweeds,
And hear the corn leaves scrape their feet on the wind.

III

Fallen ears are lying on the dusty earth.
The useful ears will lie dry in cribs, but the others, missed
By the picker, will lie here touching the ground the whole
    winter.

IV

Snow will come, and cover the husks of the fallen ears
With flakes infinitely delicate, like jewels of a murdered
    Gothic prince
Which were lost centuries ago during a great battle.

Here is another poem, called "Thinking of Robert Bly and
James Wright on the First Hot Day in April After Having
Stayed up Late All Night Drinking and Singing With a Gang
of Old Norwegian Trolls." (Bly is Norwegian.)

Whenever I think of you,
Tiny white horses gallop away in darkness.
I am lulled by the sound of old guitars
Strummed by ghostly fingers of the wind.

Your gentleness is like beautiful white snow
Drifting down on ancient homesteads
Over lonely prairies in Tennessee;
And you are falling, falling softly down.

America is falling also
Into dark cathedrals of the sea.

> But what is that to me?
> I am oblivious to missile siloes in Minnesota.
>
> I lie here in the holy darkness
> Listening to cornstalks creaking,
> Thinking I have ruined myself
> Climbing over a pale barbed-wire fence.

Now, though this latter poem is a conscious parody—it came to me in the mail the other day—the writer said he turned it out, without changing a word, as fast as he could type. Though, as I say, it is a parody, it really isn't, for it is completely undistinguishable from the seriously intended poems it models itself on. It has the same particular faults and characteristics as its models: the sentimentality, the attempt to link up all sorts of disparate items—snow, corn, jewels of murdered princes, missile siloes, and so on —in a kind of loose emotional mental drifting having a bogus, unearned conclusion. The parody is as good and as bad as the original. Above all, it is as arbitrary. This is essentially a derivative, imitative, extremely lazy, unimaginative poetry: small, static, and very easy to write. It lacks *necessity* of statement; it cannot sustain narrative. If the salvation of American poetry is to write imitation Spanish poems, even that will have to be done better than this. But no such salvation is indicated, even if it were possible. We have a lot more going for us than that.

Up to now, I have been sort of taking inventory of the extant poetries: the movements, the kinds of writing that we have among us now. As may be evident, I don't care much for any of these. I've been dwelling among the empirical evidence up to now, with some admiration but mainly indifference and some distaste. Let me now go on and develop what I think should happen, and with luck, *will* happen.

First of all, let me read something. It is by Randall Jarrell, who is going to be—if indeed he isn't already—a hero to us.

Moving from Cheer to Joy, from Joy to All,
I take a box
And add it to my wild rice, my Cornish game hens.
The slacked or shorted, basketed, identical
Food-gathering flocks
Are selves I overlook. Wisdom, said William James,

Is learning what to overlook. And I am wise
If that is wisdom.
Yet somehow, as I buy All from these shelves
And the boy takes it to my station wagon,
What I've become
Troubles me even if I shut my eyes.

When I was young and miserable and pretty
And poor, I'd wish
What all girls wish: to have a husband,
A house and children. Now that I'm old, my wish
Is womanish:
That the boy putting groceries in my car

See me. It bewilders me he doesn't see me.

Now this has its faults. Like much of Jarrell's work, it
is somewhat flat. But it does have the quality that I'd like
to see become dominant in the poetry that is forthcoming:
It is convincing as speech before it is convincing—or even
felt—as "Art," as poetry. One *believes* it, and therefore the
poem can act either as human communication or poetry, or
both, without the reader's having to kill off one side of
his receptiveness so that the other can operate. Further, this
passage has what I can only describe as a kind of *folk* quality
to it. Some of Jarrell's work is folk—or folksy—in the bad
sense, for it is self-consciously so, but the best of it is not.
And oddly enough, even in our computerized age, this offers
a direction of which we have never—but should have—
thought. For what do we mean by folk, leaving aside for
the moment considerations of the connections between a folk

idiom and the cultural environment from which it arises? Do we not mean a body of linguistic forms, of music, of crafts, customs, and so on, immediately accessible to the sensibilities of those from whom they arise? Recognizable as the language one speaks? And in poetry and balladry, for example, that language heightened but still recognizable as ours? Now this is very general, so far, but when we apply it to, say, a particular locality, it begins to make sense.

This is a short poem by Eleanor Ross Taylor, a Southern poet, and it is called "Motherhood, 1880."

> When Dave got up and struck a light
> We'd neither of us slept all night.
> We kept the fire and watched by May,
> Sick for fear she might
>
> Go off like little Tom. . . . They say
> "Don't fret . . . another on the way. . . ."
> They know I favor this least child.
>
> No use to cry. But while
> I made a fire in the kitchen stove
> I heard a pesky mourning dove.
> Lor! What's he calling "O-love" for?

And here is the last stanza of a poem called "After the Late Lynching" by Katherine Hoskins, a poet usually cited for her difficulty, but one also capable of speaking with utter directness.

> Nor not from whitest light of foreign poems
>   Hope help;
>   But from her native woe
>   Who took that black head in her hands
>   And felt,
>   "A sack of little bones";
>   Whose arms for the last time round him knew,
>   "All down one side no ribs
>   But broken things that moved."

Now these two poems are by highly sophisticated women, but it seems to me that they have been able to get back through the sophistication to something that sophistication does not usually afford: to a sense of the absolute basics of life, and for these the language of Eliot and Empson is not right. For this kind of poetry needs nothing more nor less than the simple language of necessity, such as would be conveyed if one caveman said to another one, "We have meat." This is not to say that poetry of this sort is incapable of more than one meaning; it is simply to say that multiplicity of reference and "richness of ambiguity" are no longer going to be the criteria by which the value of poetry is measured.

This kind of simplicity, which Mr. McLuhan might call "tribal"—and if he wouldn't, I would—takes a great many forms. The interesting thing about it to me is that the essential folk quality—sometimes attached to a region and sometimes not—doesn't seem to encroach on the individual poets' particular kinds of vision at all. Here, for example, is a stanza from "In Medias Res" by William Stafford, who is basically a Midwesterner, though he lives in Oregon.

> On Main one night when they sounded the chimes
> my father was ahead in shadow, my son
> behind coming into the streetlight, on each side
> a brother and a sister; and overhead
> the chimes went arching for the perfect sound.
> There was a one-stride god on Main that night,
> all walkers in a cloud.

An interesting variation of this developing approach is a kind of poetry of what I'd be tempted to call the "domestic imagination," or the poetry of the everyday nightmare, the quotidian. Allen Tate once remarked that he thought of his poems as comments on those human situations from which there is no escape. Well, there is no escape from the toothbrush and the rug that is wearing thin, or from the mirror in the hall and the dripping faucet. The best of these poets is a youngish fellow named Vern Rutsala, and I'll read one of his poems because I think you ought to know something about him. This is called "Sunday."

> Up early while everyone sleeps,
> I wander through the house,
> pondering the eloquence
> of vacant furniture, listening
> to birdsong peeling
> the cover off the day.
>
> I think everyone I know
> is sleeping now. Sidewalks
> are cool, waiting for
> roller skates and wagons.
> Skate keys are covered
> with dew; bicycles look
> broken, abandoned on the lawns—
> no balance left in them,
> awkward as wounded
> animals. I am the last
> man and this is my
> last day; I can't think
> of anything to do. Somewhere
> over my shoulder a jet
> explores a crease
> in the cloudy sky;
> I sit on the porch
> waiting for things to happen.
>
> O fat god of Sunday
> and chocolate bars, watcher
> over picnics and visits to the zoo,
> will anyone wake up today?

It has been argued for years that ours is a complex age, and a complex age calls for—no, demands—a complex poetry.

This seems to me to display what logicians call the analogical error. I think that the poetry of the future is going to go back the other way, back toward basic things and basic-sounding statements about them, in an effort, perhaps a desperate one, to get back wholeness of being, to respond fullheartedly and fullbodiedly to experience, aware all the time that certain constants must be affirmed, or not much of life will be worth anything. The great thing about poetry has always been that it can speak to people deeply about matters of genuine concern. Some of this feeling has been lost since the ascendancy of Pound and Eliot, and the poem has become a kind of high-cult *objet d'art*, a "superior amusement" as Eliot once termed it. I believe that the true poets of the future will repudiate that notion absolutely, and try to operate in that place where, as Katherine Anne Porter says, one lives "deeply and consistently in that un-distracted center of being where the will does not intrude, and the sense of time passing is lost, or has no power over the imagination." And if we are lucky in this search, and believe in it enough, we shall at least arrive at a condition of emotional primitivism, of undivided response, a condition where we can connect with whatever draws us. Walter Pater, of all people, wrote something about Wordsworth that bears on what I am saying.

> And so it came about that this sense of a life, a living soul, in natural objects, which in most poetry is but a rhetorical artifice, is with Wordsworth the assertion of what for him is almost literal fact. To him every natural object seemed to possess more or less of a moral or spiritual life—to be capable of a companionship with humanity full of expression, of inexplicable affinities, and delicacies of intercourse. An emanation, a partic-ular spirit, belonged not to the moving leaves or water only, but to the distant peak arising suddenly, by some change of perspective, above the nearer horizon of the hills, to the passing space of light across the plain, to

the lichened Druidic stone even, for a certain weird
fellowship in it with the moods of men. It was like a
survival, in the peculiar intellectual temperament of a
man of letters at the end of the eighteenth century, of
that primitive condition which some philosophers have
traced in the general history of human culture, in which
all outward objects alike, including even the works of
men's hands, were believed to be endowed with anima-
tion, and the world seemed "full of souls."

Now, we don't live in Wordsworth's age, or Pater's, but
an attitude of mind—a kind of *being*—like Wordsworth's is
no more impossible to us than it was to him. Theodore
Roethke, the greatest poet we have ever had in this country,
is a marvelous proof of this.

I, who came back from the depths laughing too loudly,
Become another thing;
My eyes extend beyond the farthest bloom of the waves;
I lose and find myself in the long water;
I am gathered together once more;
I embrace the world.

That is what we want: to be gathered together once more,
to be able to enter in, to participate in experience, to possess
our lives. I think that the new poetry will be a poetry of the
dazzlingly simple statement, the statement that is clairvoyantly
and stunningly simple but not simple in the manner of, say,
greeting cards: a stark, warm simplicity of vision: the sim-
plicity that opens out deeper into the world and carries us
with it. For we are not condemned to division within our-
selves by the world we have made for ourselves. We have
one self that is conditioned, all right. But there is another
self that has never heard of an automobile or a telephone.
This is the one that connects most readily with the flow of
rivers and the light coming from the sun; it is in this second
(or first) and infinitely older being that we can be trans-
figured by eyes and recreated by flesh. We can participate

in a "survival" (in Pater's terms), a certain animism. As Camus says as he eats a peach (he *does* dare to eat a peach!):

> My teeth close on the peach. I hear the great strokes of my blood rise into my ears. I look with all of my eyesight. On the sea is the enormous silence of noon. Every beautiful being and thing has the natural pride of its beauty, and the world today lets its pride leak away everywhere. But before this world, why should I deny myself the joy of being alive, even if I can't close this joy up and keep it? There is no shame in being happy. But today the imbecile is king, and I call the imbecile that man who is afraid of joy.

It can begin—a poem, a true life—with something that simple. We need that worse than we need anything else: not sensation, but feeling; mainly the feeling of ourselves. And any poetry that I want to read in the future will find its own way of conveying this basic, this irreducible sense of being.

And—who knows? Maybe at some undetermined time in the future, encompassed around by Marshall McLuhan's world of telemetry and computers, his "instantaneous world" of electronic circuitry, in that place he calls "the global village" and "the retribalized society," we shall again have a purely tribal poetry, something naive and utterly convincing, immediately accessible, animistic, communal, dancelike, entered into, participated in. We are not Eskimos or Bantus, and our "global village" is immeasurably different from one composed of igloos or thatched huts, but if McLuhan is right—and I think he is more right than wrong—and if *I* am right, we may live to see the day that our poetry has the simplicity, though not the subject matter, of this, from an un-McLuhan-type tribe of Eskimos in northern Canada:

> Glorious it is
> To see long-haired winter caribou
> Returning to the forests.

Fearfully they watch
For the little people.
While the herd follows the ebb-mark of the sea
With a storm of clattering hooves.
Glorious it is
When wandering time is come.

And with this "second being"—the part of us that the light
of the sun moves without our having thoughts of "harness-
ing its energy" or using it in any way—we will write the
poetry that I want most to read and hear. As Richard Jef-
feries so magnificently says:

The mind must acknowledge its ignorance; all the learning
and lore of so many eras must be erased from it as
an encumbrance. It is not from past or present knowl-
edge, science or faith, that it is to be drawn. Erase these
altogether as they are erased under the fierce heat of
the focus before me. Begin wholly afresh. Go straight
to the sun, the immense forces of the universe, to the
Entity unknown; go higher than a god; deeper than
prayer; and open a new day.

And finally it may be, if this is indeed a real trend I
describe, that we shall get back even farther than the poetry
of the tribe and reach all the way to the very root-beginnings,
back to the state of mind of the first man himself, who
stood on the shore and opened his arms to the world, that
he and the world might possess each other. Let me end by
quoting part of a wonderful poem by Brewster Ghiselin
called "The Vision of Adam." As Adam swims in the sea
to try to discover his origin, he discovers instead the divine
sensuality of the world, where the spirit of each of us
hides and waits for each of us to come.

> And over the empty ocean the rose
> and amber

Paled slowly and without sorrow, and ever more faintly
                gleamed
About the increase of a western star. Adam swimming
In the chill water loved the cold and the menace.
He felt vast depth beneath him, and looking back
Saw the faint shore and heard far off the murmur of anger
                beginning
On the benighted sand, under wind and falling foam.
"It is not vision, but life, I want," said Adam,
"The power of the sea." A wave filled his mouth
 With keen salt. The wind of evening gathered the wide billows
                beyond the last kelp
Into mounds with soft ripples crowning delicately
The long slopes with the sweetness of water released from
                the parent urge.
And Adam ceased swimming, and floated over darkness
                beyond the kelp
Which makes a seamark for swimmers, and watched how
                the stars
Came to the open pool of the central azure.
And he thought nothing at all, but felt the incalculable power
                of the ocean
Cradled upon the foundations of the world, and moving to
                the unspeaking moon.

Adam idly, in the black water, turned and swam shoreward
Past the place where the sea stars are lonelier
Than the stars of the land. He swam on his back
Through thick kelp: sea-shine clinging
On the long leaves ground fire against motion.
Then, swimming through clear water, he looked up
And saw the seaward stars:
The Scorpion in a bright anguish coiled on a bed of sea mist,
And where the split sky-stream divided light above the ocean,
Sagittarius, the Archer, the dancing rider, in a faint snow
              of stars. And still he swam

And was not as nothing beneath the tyranny of all that
        splendor,
Nor poured out like starlight in wonder along the ocean.
        Yet the mystery of the stars,
Darker than night wind in spring, and more strange with
        secrets,
Was present as he swam, and was like a wind
Freshening the world.

TWO VOICES

1 EDWIN ARLINGTON ROBINSON

Poetic fashions, like other kinds, change; that we all know. But the lives of poets change, too, in our eyes. One kind of life—one life—interests us, and then, for our own reasons or reasons connected with how we all live, another. We think for a while that the only real poet is the roaring boy or the criminal-*voyant*, but finally we must turn from him, for what of the strange, quiet poet who sees not "a thousand white angels on the road" but a man and woman who hate each other but won't give each other up?

And so there is a new interest in the life as well as the poetry of Edwin Arlington Robinson, the most easily ignored of men until you are hit by the full import of the words you must strain to hear. Chard Powers Smith's fine "Where the Light Falls" of 1965 is a case in point, as is the late Morton Dauwen Zabel's new selection of the same year, and as are the critical studies of Edwin Fussell and W. R. Robinson and the older one of Yvor Winters.

And now we have Louis Coxe's short, sharp critical biography as further evidence of the discreet fascination that the man's work has for a good many of us, as well as of the increasing fascination of his mysterious and perhaps unfathomable personality.

In a world in which the main things—both the best and the worst but in any event the most necessary things—are the interactions between human beings, Robinson looms in a shadowy but very large way, as exactly the kind of poet we cannot elude. He has little eye for nature, little or no interest in stylistic experimentation, in writing immortal lines, in most of the characteristics that we commonly have been led to associate with the composition of poetry. He doesn't write like a demon or a god; he writes like a man, saying what you and I would say about the people we know, if we knew the way to say it, and if we had the nerve to tell the truth; that is, if we *cared* enough.

Mr. Coxe understands this exactly. His defense of the plain, "average-man" style of Robinson is the best such defense I know. As he says, Robinson "extended the range of what poetry can talk about," and in his discussions of *how* Robinson talked about his sad clerks and doctors of billiards, his derelicts-with-genius and bastard sailors and ancient whores and grief-stricken butchers, he shows us more than we had known about the strange, anonymous kind of poet-observer Robinson is—not God-like but human and having to bear the same limitations as his subjects—as he "prowls around the edges of the action and overhears and ponders and judges, or perhaps fails to decide."

Coxe also brilliantly demonstrates how Robinson's unemphatic, anti-rhetorical style drives the nail of conviction into the reader's skull. The best of his poems are terribly painful, and they are so simply because we believe them; we believe this really happened to someone, and that it happend pretty much as Robinson says it did.

> For when they told him that his wife must die,
> He stared at them, and shook with grief and fright,
> And cried like a great baby half that night,
> And made the women cry to see him cry.

Though this is unmistakably poetry, it is not "doctored"; literature has not been worrying at it in its usual ways and making it self-conscious; in short, it is believable, as most poetry is not.

How did this man hit on such a way of doing things, which is the easiest possible one to conceive of—the first one that poetry ought to concern itself with—and the hardest to achieve? That, of course, is the story of Robinson's life. Always odd and self-effacing and immovable, he saw his Maine family fall apart around him, his adored brother Dean become a narcotics addict, his mother die of "black diphtheria" in a scene far surpassing in New England gothic anything in Eugene O'Neill: "No one—doctor, pastor, undertaker—would enter the house. Her sons ministered to her, the parson said a prayer through the window, the undertaker left a coffin on the porch, and the three brothers buried their mother in the graveyard . . ." He spent most of the rest of his life "as an outcast on the fringes of New York Bohemia, without wife, child, or relation of any kind, except his nieces back in Gardiner, a town he no doubt wished he could forget. . . ."

But he couldn't, and the poems came to him from there, from Gardiner, the "Tilbury Town" of his first good writing. And the manner those poems gave him he applied to subjects drawn from New York, which he characteristically referred to as "the town down the river," and then to Camelot, Elizabethan England, and other places, all very like Gardiner. But this similarity did not bother him, as it really does not bother us, for he deals far more with the constants of human behavior—despair, failure and uncertainty—than he does with the accidents and appearances of particular times and places.

Robinson more than any other is the poet of secret lives, and of actions that are the results of motivations hard or impossible to guess, or even to guess at. He is a psychological poet in a very special sense, a poet of the misspent life and the missed opportunity, of the bafflement of decision-making and the regrets over those made.

The unspoken question in almost every Robinson poem is

"Why is it this way?" What did I do wrong? Was there ever a right I could have done? And if I did, would it matter? Why has this happened to me? To Reuben Bright? Why has his wife died, so that all he can do is go helplessly down to the slaughterhouse and tear it apart? Why is Luke Havergal called to "the western gate?" Why is Time "so vicious in his reaping?" Why are the games of Time "played like this?"

Answers, answers. *What* answers? If it is true that every poet desires to be "master of a superior secret," and if we apply this to Robinson, we would be forced to say that his secret is that there *is* no secret, no answer. One cannot, finally, judge; one can only present. And that is what Robinson does. His compassion is everywhere evident, but he does not insist on it.

One can imagine this vulnerable, quiet man wherever he is imaginable—wherever Mr. Coxe has imagined him: in Gardiner, in New York, at the MacDowell Colony—sitting in a chair staring at his own nondescript image in the mirror, his eyes fiery with unwitnessed crying, his knuckles at his lips, asking questions about himself, about other people, and getting nothing back. It is harrowing. Most of us think, now and then, that there aren't any answers, but Robinson *knows* there aren't. That is because he has asked for them more deeply than we have, and has suffered more at being denied them, or at being ignored.

He is a writer of immense power, of power on the tangent, the elliptical, the circular. He shows the million ways in which the suffering human creature is trapped among the tangle of his choices, and haunted by the possibilities of what those choices have made forever irrecoverable. The Robinson Man is like an animal in the endless trap of his own mind, the web of decisions and consequences, all presided over by Time, which never heals and never corrects. We must reckon with him, for we cannot escape.

2 THE GREATEST AMERICAN POET: ROETHKE

Once there were three men in the living room of an apartment in Seattle. Two of them were present in body, watching each other with the wariness of new acquaintance, and the other was there by telephone. The two in Carolyn Kizer's apartment were Theodore Roethke and I, and the voice was Allan Seager in Michigan. All three had been drinking, I the most, Roethke the next most, and Seager, apparently, the least. After a long-distance joke about people I had never heard of, Roethke said, "Allan, I want you to meet a friend of mine. He's a great admirer of yours, by the way."

I picked up the phone and said, according to conviction and opportunity, "This is Charles Berry."

"This is *who?*"

"Your son, Amos. Charles Berry, the poet."

"The *hell* it is!"

"I thought you might like to know what happened to Charles after the end of the novel. In one way or the other, he became me. My name is James Dickey."

"Well, thanks for telling me. But I had other plans for Charles. Maybe even using him in another novel. I think he did finally become a poet. But not you."

"No, no; it's a joke."

"I had it figured. But it ain't funny."

"Sorry," I said. "I meant it as a kind of tribute, I guess."

"Well, thanks, I guess."

"Joke or not, I think your book *Amos Berry* is a great novel."

"I do too, but nobody else does. It's out of print, with the rest of my stuff."

"Listen," I said, trying to get into the phone, "I doubt if I'd've tried to be a poet if it weren't for Charles Berry. There was no call for poetry in my background, any more than there was in his. But he wanted to try, and he kept on with it. So I did, too."

"How about Amos? What did you think of him?"

"I like to think he's possible. My God! A middle-aged businessman trying to kick off all of industrial society! Get rid of the whole of Western civilization and go it on his own!"

"Yeah, but he failed."

"He failed, but it was a failure that mattered. And the scenes after the rebellious poet-son meets the rebellious father who's just killed his employer and gotten away with it—well, that's a *meeting!* And Amos turns out to be proud of his boy, who's doing this equally insane thing of writing poetry. Right?"

"Sure. Sure he's proud. Like many another, when the son has guts and does something strange and true to what he is. Say, is Ted Roethke still around there?"

"Yes. He's right here. Want to speak to him?"

"No; but he's another one. He's one of those sons. But his father didn't live long enough to know it."

That was my introduction to Allan Seager, a remarkable man and a writer whose works—*Equinox, The Inheritance, Amos Berry, Hilda Manning, The Old Man of the Mountain, The Death of Anger, A Frieze of Girls*—will, as Henry James said of his own, "kick off their tombstones" time after time, in our time and after. His last book and his only biography, *The Glass House* (McGraw-Hill, $6.95), is this

life of Roethke, who is in my opinion the greatest poet this
country has yet produced.

During his life and after his death in 1963, people interested
in poetry heard a great many rumors about Roethke. Most of
these had to do with his eccentricities, his periodic insanity,
his drinking, his outbursts of violence, his unpredictability.
He came to be seen as a self-destructive American genius
somewhat in the pattern of Dylan Thomas. Roethke had a
terrifying half-tragic, half-low-comedy life out of which he
lifted, by the strangest and most unlikely means, and by
endless labors and innumerable false starts, the poetry that all
of us owe it to ourselves to know and cherish. If Beethoven
said, "He who truly understands my music can never know
unhappiness again," Roethke's best work says with equal au-
thority, "He who truly opens himself to my poems will
never again conceive his earthly life as worthless."

The Glass House is the record—no, the story, for Seager's
novelistic talents give it that kind of compellingness—of how
such poetry as Roethke's came to exist. It was written by a
man who battled for his whole adult life against public in-
difference to novels and stories he knew were good, and
fought to his last conscious hour to finish this book. Some
time after meeting him by telephone, which was in the spring
of 1963, I came to know him better, and two summers ago
spent a week with him in Tecumseh, Michigan. Most of that
time we talked about the biography and about Roethke, and
went over the sections he had completed. From the first few
words Seager read me, I could tell that this was no *mere*
literary biography; there was too much of a sense of personal
identification between author and subject to allow for mere-
ness. Seager said to me, in substance, what he had written to a
friend some time before this:

> Beatrice Roethke, the widow of Thedore Roethke, has
> asked me to write the authorized life of her husband.
> I was in college with him and knew him fairly intimately

the rest of his life. It is a book I'd like to do. Quite aside from trying to evoke the character that made the poetry, there are a good many things to say about the abrasion of the artist in America that he exemplifies. We were both born in Michigan, he in Saginaw, I in Adrian. We both came from the same social stratum. Much of his life I have acted out myself.

Though Seager did not witness the whole process of Roethke's development, not having known the poet in his childhood, he did see a great deal of it, and the told me that he had seen what happened to Roethke happen "in an evolutionary way." More than once he said, "Ted started out as a phony and became genuine, like Yeats." And, "I had no idea that he'd end up as fine a poet as he did. No one knew that in the early days, Ted least of all. We all knew he *wanted* to be a great poet or a great something, but to a lot of us that didn't seem enough. I could have told you, though, that his self-destructiveness would get worse. I could have told you that awful things were going to happen to him. He was headed that way; at times he seemed eager to speed up the process."

I saw Roethke only twice myself. I saw only a sad fat man who talked continually of joy, and although I liked him well enough for such a short acquaintance, came away from him each time with a distinct sense of relief. Like everyone else who knew him even faintly, I was pressed into service in the cause of his ego, which reeled and tottered pathetically at all hours and under all circumstances, and required not only props, but the *right* props. What did I think of Robert Lowell, Randall Jarrell, and "the Eastern literary gang"? What did I think of the "gutless Limey reviewers" in the *Times Literary Supplement?* I spent an afternoon with him trying to answer such questions, before giving a reading at the University of Washington. Carolyn Kizer, an old friend and former student of Roethke's, had given a party the day before the reading, and I was introduced to Roethke there. Though

I had heard various things about him, ranging from the need to be honest with him to the absolute need *not* to be honest, I was hardly prepared for the way in which, as Southerners used to say, he "carried on." I was identified in his mind only as the man who had said (in the *Virginia Quarterly Review*, to be exact) that he was the greatest poet then writing in English. He kept getting another drink and bringing me one and starting the conversation over from that point, leading (more or less naturally for him, I soon discovered) into a detailed and meticulously quoted list of what other poets and critics had said about him. I got the impression that my name was added to those of Auden, Stanley Kunitz, Louise Bogan, and Rolfe Humphries not because I was in any way as distinguished in Roethke's mind as they were, but because I had provided him with a kind of *climactic* comment: something he needed that these others hadn't quite managed to say, at least in print. And later, when he introduced me at the reading, he began with the comment, and talked for eight or ten minutes about himself, occasionally mentioning me as though by afterthought. I did not resent this, though I found it curious, and I bring it up now only to call attention to qualities that must have astonished and confounded others besides myself.

Why should a poet of Roethke's stature conduct himself in this childish and embarrassing way? Why all this insistence on being the best, the acknowledged best, the *written-up* best? Wasn't the poetry itself enough? And why the really appalling pettiness about other writers, like Lowell, who were not poets to him but rivals merely? There was never a moment that I was with Roethke when I was not conscious of something like this going on in his mind; never a moment when he did not have the look of a man fighting for his life in some way known only to him. The strain was in the very air around him; his broad, babyish face had an expression of constant bewilderment and betrayal, a continuing agony of doubt. He seemed to cringe and brace himself at the same time. He would glare from the corners of his eyes and turn wordlessly away. Then he would enter into a long involved story about himself. "I used to spar with Steve Hamas," he would say. I remember trying to remember who Steve Hamas was, and by the time I had faintly conjured up an American heavyweight who was knocked out by Max Schmeling, Roethke was glaring at me anxiously. "What the hell's wrong?" he said. "You think I'm a damned liar?"

I did indeed, but until he asked me, I thought he was just rambling on in the way of a man who did not intend for others to take him seriously. He *seemed* serious enough, for he developed the stories at great length, as though he had told them, to others or to himself, a good many times before. Such a situation puts a stranger in rather a tough spot. If he suspects that the story is a lie, he must either pretend to go along with it, or hopefully enter a tacit conspiracy with the speaker in assuming that the whole thing is a joke, a put-on. Unfortunately I chose the latter, and I could not have done worse for either of us. He sank, or fell, rather, into a steep and bitter silence—we were driving around Seattle at the time—and there was no more said on that or any other subject until we reached his house on John Street. I must have been awfully slow to catch on to what he wanted of me, for in retrospect it seems quite clear that he wished me to help protect him from his sense of inadequacy, his dissatisfaction with what he was as a man.

My own disappointment, however, was not at all in the *fact* that Roethke lied, but in the obviousness and uncreativeness of the manner in which he did it. Lying of an inspired, habitual, inventive kind, given a personality, a form, and a rhythm, is mainly what poetry *is*, I have always believed. All art, as Picasso is reported to have said, is a lie that makes us see the truth. There are innumerable empirical "truths" in the world—billions a day, an hour, a minute—but only a few poems that surpass and transfigure them: only a few structures of words which do not so much tell the truth as *make* it. I would have found Roethke's lies a good deal more memorable if they had had some of the qualities of his best poems, and had not been simply the productions of the grown-up baby that he resembled physically. Since that time I have much regretted that Roethke did not write his prize-fighting poems, his gangster poems and tycoon poems, committing his art to these as fully as he committed himself to them in conversation. This might have given his work the range and variety of subject matter that it so badly needed, particularly toward the end of his life, when he was beginning to repeat himself: they might have been the themes to make of him a poet of the stature of Yeats or Rilke.

Yet this is only speculation; his poems are as we have them, and many of them will be read as long as words retain the power to evoke a world and to relate the reader, through that world, to a more intense and meaningful version of his own. There is no poetry anywhere that is so valuably conscious of the human body as Roethke's; no poetry that can place the body in an *environment*—wind, seascape, greenhouse, forest, desert, mountainside, among animals or insects or stones—so vividly and evocatively, waking unheard of exchanges between the place and human responsiveness at its most creative. He more than any other is a poet of pure being. He is a great poet not because he tells you how it is with *him* —as, for example, the "confessional" poets endlessly do—but how it can be with you. When you read him, you realize with a great surge of astonishment and joy that, truly, you are not yet dead.

Roethke came to possess this ability slowly. *The Glass House* is like a long letter by a friend, telling how he came to have it. The friend's concern and occasional bewilderment about the subject are apparent, and also some of the impatience that Roethke's self-indulgent conduct often aroused even in those closest to him. But the main thrust of his life, his emergence from Saginaw, Michigan (of all places), into the heroic role of an artist working against the terrible odds of himself for a new vision, is always clear; clearer than it ever was to Roethke, who aspired to self-transcendence but continually despaired of attaining it.

Herioc Roethke certainly was; he struggled against more than most men are aware is possible. His guilt and panic never left him. No amount of praise could ever have been enough to reassure him or put down his sense of chagrin and bafflement over his relationship to his father, the florist Otto Roethke, who died early in Roethke's life and so placed himself beyond reconciliation. None of his lies—of being a nationally ranked tennis player, of having an "in" with the Detroit "Purple Gang," of having all kinds of high-powered business interests and hundreds of women in love with him —would ever have shriven him completely, but these lures and ruses and deceptions did enable him to exist, though painfully, and to write; they were the paraphernalia of the wounded artist who cannot survive without them.

These things Seager deals with incisively and sympathetically. He is wonderful on the genesis of the poetry, and his accounts of Roethke's greatest breakthrough, the achievement of what Kenneth Burke calls his "greenhouse line," are moving indeed, and show in astonishing detail the extent to which Roethke lived his poems and identified his bodily existence with them in one animistic rite after another.

On days when he was not teaching, he moped around Shingle Cottage alone, scribbling lines in his notebooks, sometimes, he told me, drinking a lot as a deliberate stimulus (later he came to see alcohol as a depressant and used to curb his manic states), popping out of his clothes, wandering around the cottage naked for a while, then dressing slowly, four or five times a day. There are some complex "birthday-suit" meanings here, the ritual of starting clean like a baby, casting one's skin like a snake, and then donning the skin again. It was not exhibitionism. No one saw. It was all a kind of magic.

He broke through to what had always been there; he discovered his childhood in a new way, and found the way to tell it, not "like it was" but as it might have been if it included all its own meanings, rhythms, and symbolic extensions. He found, in other words, the form for it: *his* form. Few writers are so obviously rooted (and in Roethke's case the word has special connotations because the poet has so magnificently put them there) in their childhood as Roethke, and Seager shows us in just what ways this was so: the authoritarian Prussian father and his specialized and exotic (especially in frozen, logged-out Saginaw) vocation of florist, the greenhouse, the "far field" behind it, the game park, the strange, irreducible life of stems and worms, the protection of fragile blooms by steam pipes, by eternal vigilance, and by getting "in there" with the plants and working with them as they not only required but seemed to want. Later there are the early efforts to write, the drinking, the first manic states, the terrible depressions, the marriage to Beatrice O'Connell (a former student of his at Bennington), the successive books, the prizes, the recognitions, the travels, the death at fifty-six.

I doubt very much if Roethke will ever have another biography as good as this one. And yet something is wrong here, even so. One senses too much of an effort to mitigate certain traits of Roethke's, particularly in regard to his relations with women. It may be argued that a number of people's feelings and privacy are being spared, and that may be, as has been adjudged in other cases, reason enough to be reticent. And yet a whole—and very important—dimension of the subject has thereby been left out of account, and one cannot help believing that a writer of Seager's ability and fierce honesty would have found a way to deal with it if he had not been constrained. To his credit, however, he does his best to suggest what he cannot overtly say. For it is no good to assert, as some have done, that Roethke was a big lovable clumsy affectionate bear who just incidentally wrote wonderful poems. It is no good to insist that Seager show "the good times as well as the bad" in anything like equal proportions; these are not the proportions of the man's life. The driving force of him was agony, and to know him we must know all the forms it took. The names of people may be concealed, but the incidents we must know. It is far worse to leave these matters to rumor than to entrust them to a man of Seager's integrity.

Mrs. Roethke, in especial, must be blamed for this wavering of purpose, this evasiveness that was so far from Seager's nature as to seem to belong to someone else. It may be that she has come to regard herself as the sole repository of the "truth" of Roethke, which is understandable as a human—particularly a wifely—attitude, but is not pardonable in one who commissions a biography from a serious writer. Allan Seager was not a lesser man than Roethke, someone to be sacrificed to another writer's already overguarded reputation. As a human being he was altogether more admirable than his subject. He was a hard and devoted worker, and he believed deeply in this book; as he said, he had acted out much of it himself. If he hadn't spent the last years of his life on *The Glass House*, he might have been able to finish the big novel he had been working on for years. As it was—thanks again to Mrs. Roethke, who, in addition to other obstacles she placed in Seager's way, even refused him permission to quote her husband's poems—he died without knowing whether all the obstacles had been removed.

Certainly this is a dreadful misplacement of loyalty, for Roethke deserves the monument that this book could have been. He had, almost exclusively by his art, all but won out over his babydom, of which this constant overprotectiveness on the part of other people was the most pernicious part. He deserved to be treated, at last, as a man as well as a great poet. And it should be in the *exact* documentation of this triumph —this heroism—that we ought to see him stand forth with no excuses made, no whitewash needed. Seager had all the gifts: the devotion to his subject, the personal knowledge of it, the talent and the patience and the honesty, and every- thing but the time and the cooperation, and above all, the recognition of his own stature as an artist with a great personal stake in the enterprise. He died of lung cancer last May.

Since I was close to the book for some time, I am bound to be prejudiced; I am glad to be. Even allowing for prejudice, however, I can still say that this is the best biography of an American poet I have read since Philip Horton's *Hart Crane*, and that it is like no other. God knows what it would have been if Allan Seager had had his way, had been able to do the job he envisioned, even as he lay dying.

ONE VOICE

One is never sure whether it is heard or overheard, whether it is saying something immortal or delusionary. It comes, mixed in with other things: clichés, other poets' good and mediocre lines, tags from newspapers and grammar school history books. It is not always unmistakable when it is heard, but there is usually, even in the first word, something arresting about it, something that has a *sound* of unusualness, of a quickening of interest in an outward part of the world. At this accent, one sits still, afraid even to move the lips, for the thread of the voice can be instantly broken, and nothing can call it back from the silence into which it has gone. At these times, hearing the voice—one's own deepest, strangest, most necessary and best voice, the voice with which one most tellingly exclaims against the void—is like wearing the earphones of an old crystal radio set, when the fragile hair of the wire is touching the pure crystal, by instants, where it lives. The sound is mainly that of static, the roaring of the void, but now and again a voice speaks clearly through it, and says something remarkable, something never before heard—or overheard—in human time. This language, this fragment which seems to belong to a larger whole that the void swallows when the crystal instantaneously converts, as it will do, from being a touchstone to common matter, is yet connected in such intimate and profound ways with what the poet really does feel about things, about his own experience and about a dreamed-of mode of speaking of it, that it appears to belong to a self other than the one which tries to articulate these experiences in poems using the ordinary means of mortal poets. It belongs, really, to a better thing, a better order of things within himself than he has yet been able to achieve.

It is the poet's sovereign challenge to make the poem rise to the level, insofar as its enveloping context and tone are concerned, of a few words overheard by chance. The poet's voice at the only time it ever really matters is the one he never suspected he had. It is his own voice when it surprises him most: when it pronounces on the events of his life as though it knew something he didn't.